PREMIER LEAGUE

CHAMPIONS

19|20

PREMIER LEAGUE

CHAMPIONS

19|20

Reach Sport

Hardback edition first published in Great Britain in 2020
www.reachsport.com
@reach_sport
Reach Sport is a part of Reach PLC Ltd, 5 St Paul's Square, Liverpool, L3 9SJ
One Canada Square, Canary Wharf, London, E15 5AP

Hardback ISBN: 9781911613756

Photographic acknowledgements:
Liverpool FC Getty Images, PA, Mirrorpix, Darcy McKellar (LMA), Jack Finnigan

Editor: David Cottrell
Design: Colin Sumpter
Production Editor: Michael McGuinness
Writers: William Hughes, Chris McLoughlin
Cover: Rick Cooke

Printed and bound by Bell & Bain

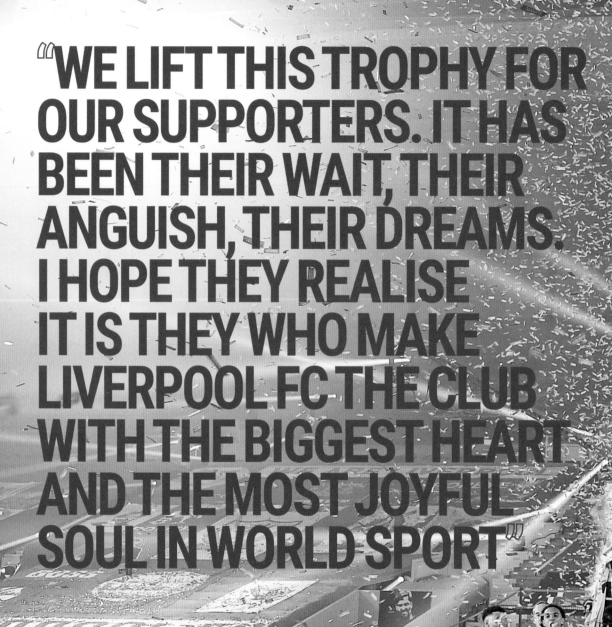

"WE LIFT THIS TROPHY FOR OUR SUPPORTERS. IT HAS BEEN THEIR WAIT, THEIR ANGUISH, THEIR DREAMS. I HOPE THEY REALISE IT IS THEY WHO MAKE LIVERPOOL FC THE CLUB WITH THE BIGGEST HEART AND THE MOST JOYFUL SOUL IN WORLD SPORT"

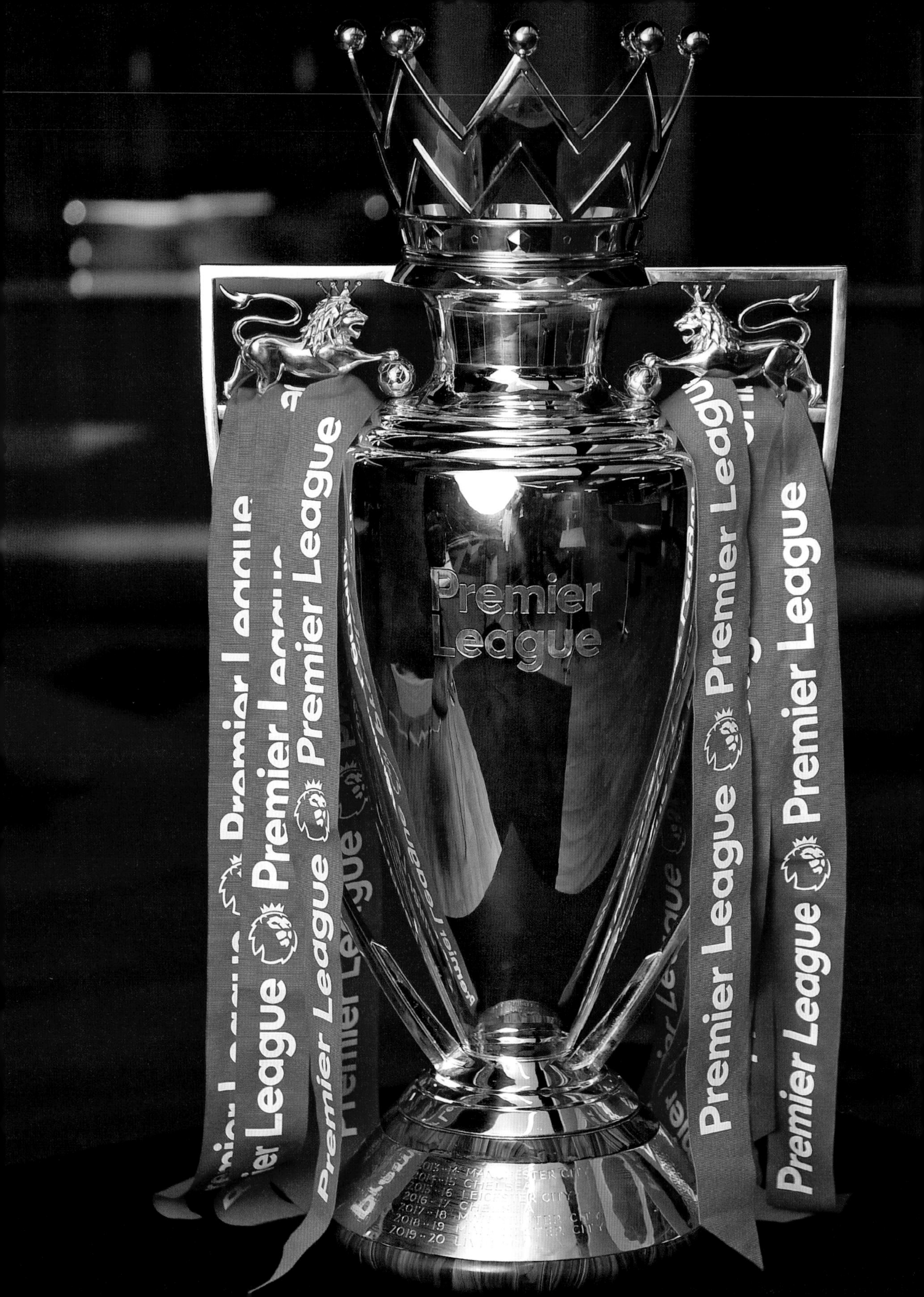
Premier League

CONTENTS
19|20

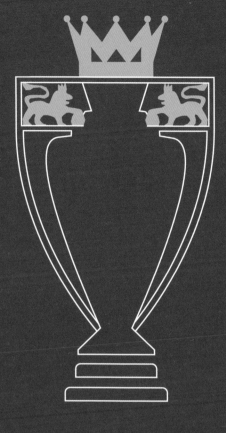

PROLOGUE

"BEING SECOND ISN'T WHAT WE WANT
– IT'S JUST A FIRST STEP"

This is the story of how Liverpool FC won the Premier League with a record-breaking seven matches to spare, surpassing their astonishing points total from the season before, in a campaign which lasted nine days short of a year and whose trophy-awarding finale was played inside an empty Anfield.

In August 2019 what were the chances of this book beginning with *that* opening line?

Back then fans were still pinching themselves after the Reds had soothed the heartache of their record-breaking runners-up spot by landing a sixth European Cup.

Liverpool had become the first team in top-flight history to win 30 games and amass 97 points and not win their domestic title, the only side to lose just one game and not be crowned champions. In manager Jürgen Klopp's book that meant just one thing: smile – and let's be even better.

"Being second isn't what we wanted but we'll take it," he said at the end of the 2018/19 Premier League season.

"This is a first step – that's how we see it."

With the triumphant Champions League final against Tottenham Hotspur in Madrid taking place on the first day of June 2019, the squad had barely a month off before the majority reported back to Melwood for pre-season training on 6 July.

The club's first summer signing, Dutch teenage centre-back Sepp van den Berg, was among them, while Alex Oxlade-Chamberlain returned after his long-term injury.

The following day goalkeeper Alisson Becker and forward Roberto Firmino won the Copa America with Brazil, beating Peru 3-1 at Rio's legendary Maracana.

Back home the boss explained what the Champions League victory would do for his players: "Of course we move on, but why should we forget it? It's something that should give the boys more confidence – that's important.

"It's not about being finally satisfied, happy or done with our careers because we won the Champions League – there is so much to go for.

"We smelled really how it feels. We played the final, we won the final, we came into the city, we saw the city and saw the people. That's something you can get addicted to, you want to have that much more often.

"It's something for the future when you look back, but while you are in your career, as we all are, you have to use it as the next basis and to start new for a completely different season."

On 11 July the Reds began their pre-season schedule with a 6-0 win at Tranmere Rovers, with young local prospect Curtis Jones among the scorers. A few days later they won 3-1 at Bradford City on a day of tribute to former defender Stephen Darby who'd been diagnosed with Motor Neurone Disease.

Then came the summer tour: three games in North America plus further matches in Edinburgh and Geneva. With several members of the senior squad only just returning from their summer international commitments, Liverpool lost 3-2 to Borussia Dortmund in Indiana and 2-1 to Sevilla at Boston's Fenway Park before drawing 2-2 with Sporting Lisbon at the Yankee Stadium in New York.

There followed a chastening 3-0 defeat by Napoli at Edinburgh's Murrayfield Stadium, with 16-year-old Harvey Elliott, whose signing from Fulham had been confirmed earlier in the day, making his debut as a second-half substitute.

A tough sequence of results, but vice-captain James Milner insisted: "We have to use it as a good thing. Dealing with games so close and all the travelling [in pre-season], it will be a piece of cake when we get one game a week at the start of the season."

Ahead of Liverpool's first appearance in the FA Community Shield for 13 years, the squad embarked on a week-long training camp in Evian in southeastern France which Klopp called "massively important. We're looking forward to it, absolutely.

"Everybody's coming back in time so Shaq [Xherdan Shaqiri], Naby [Keita], Bobby [Firmino], Mo [Salah] and Alisson [Becker] will be in training, which is great."

The Reds rounded off their pre-season fixture-list with a 3-1 win over Lyon in Geneva, then headed home to the announcement that Melwood had been acquired by a not-for-profit, affordable housing provider.

It meant that 2019/20 was scheduled to be the last season at their famous training-base before they moved to a new, state-of-the-art facility in Kirkby.

So to Wembley and the season curtain-raiser against Manchester City, the team which had denied Liverpool that elusive first title of the Premier League era.

Ex-Reds attacker Raheem Sterling put City in front but Joel Matip headed Liverpool level. It went to a shootout and the Reds went down 5-4 on spot-kicks.

Defender Trent Alexander-Arnold took plenty of positives from Liverpool's performance, having represented the Reds at the national stadium for the first time.

"It was disappointing not to get the trophy at the end

of the day because we probably deserved it for our second-half performance," was his assessment.

"We were outstanding and showed signs that we will be as good, if not better, this season."

Talk about prescient. City had taken the honours again this time but the Reds remained resolute.

There was also a flurry of late transfer activity at Anfield, mostly of the outgoing variety with younger players moving on permanently or as loans.

The major business saw keeper Simon Mignolet leave for FC Bruges after six seasons with the club.

Later that same day Liverpool announced the signing of former West Ham United goalie Adrian on a free transfer.

So, no big incoming additions to a first-team squad which the manager trusted implicitly to embrace the challenge and play with big hearts and a passion for winning.

With the hard yards well and truly put in, the Reds were ready to go.

Sitting comfortably? Good, because you might not quite believe what's about to happen...

1

STRONGER, FITTER, SMARTER

After a summer which had seen fellow headline acts like Take That, Bon Jovi and Pink play at Anfield, the mighty Reds were ready to return to their beloved home for the first time since being crowned champions of Europe – and Liverpool's 2019/20 Premier League campaign started with a Friday-night game against newly-promoted Norwich City. It was warm(ish), it was light. It felt good to be a Red.

As anticipation built ahead of the big kick-off, club chief-executive Peter Moore underlined the club's ambition: "We enjoyed a magical end to the 2018/19 season and have no intention of standing still."

A handful of Jürgen Klopp's squad received eve-of-season boosts with Alisson Becker, Trent Alexander-Arnold, Virgil van Dijk, Jordan Henderson and Sadio Mane all being shortlisted for UEFA's 2018/19 positional Champions League awards.

Mane had returned to training at Melwood on Monday 5 August, the day after the FA Community Shield, having had a very short spell of rest and recovery following his endeavours at the Africa Cup of Nations with Senegal, whom he'd helped reach the final against Algeria on 19 July.

Most of the pre-season previews in the media talked up another close title race and predicted another second-placed finish for the Reds behind Manchester City. The bookmakers tended to agree, with 5-2 being the sort of price offered on Liverpool ending a 30-year wait for their 19th top-flight championship.

Guardian journalist Andy Hunter, though, just had a hunch: "Waiting for the champions to falter [last season] during an enthralling run-in proved punishing and futile for Liverpool [and] it may do so again this season. Yet their appetite has been whetted by a sixth European crown. They look the only team capable of denying Manchester City a Premier League hat-trick.

"Liverpool have progressed each season under Klopp, but improving on a club-record points tally plus the ultimate triumph in Madrid presents a formidable challenge for the manager who has unified Anfield."

The disappointment of losing out to City in that unbelievable 2018/19 race still lingered, but Virgil van Dijk had sent this clear message in the aftermath of the glory that was Madrid: "This is just the start. It's not like we're going away."

Klopp had also received a phone-call from City manager Pep Guardiola offering his congratulations following that historic triumph over Tottenham Hotspur. "We promised each other that we will kick each other's butts again next season!" revealed the Reds boss. "We will go for everything and see what we get."

And with the preliminaries over, Klopp was typically rousing in his must-read matchday programme notes for the opening game against the Canaries: "A new season is always about opportunity. I think this coming one presents the best kind of opportunity for all of us in the LFC fold.

"As the team, we know we have the opportunity to be better than we were last season. This I love about football. Regardless of what came before you know there are new challenges and new memories to make.

"This team, since I have been fortunate enough to lead them, has been all about progression collectively and individually. They know standing still means you actually fall backwards.

"In the Premier League, the domestic cups and Europe, all our opponents will make strides forward. Our strides

can and must be bigger if we want to achieve.

"I hear the words often – after a season like we just had – about how difficult or how important it is to 'go again'. I don't dislike the sentiment and there is merit to it, but simply 'going again' won't be enough. We need to be even stronger, even fitter, smarter, more committed, greater focus.

"Maybe a slight change on the sentiment: 'improve again', maybe 'progress again'. But it's the challenge that makes it so fulfilling and so enjoyable."

He also touched on the importance of the Anfield faithful and the need to enjoy the challenges the season presented together: "Let's never lose sight of what we are all involved in. It's about energy and joy. It's about shared experiences. There is so much in the outside world that is not to enjoy at the moment, so much that is divisive.

"Football – at its best – is the antidote to this, albeit we know it can only often be brief respite.

"Football offers the chance for people from all backgrounds and all communities to come together and focus on achieving something amazing through collective effort. Everyone – from the players, to the staff, to the supporters – share equally in the joyous moment of a goal or a win.

"We can all experience the fulfilment that comes from helping each other. Supporters give energy to the players through atmosphere and players give energy

back through their commitment and enterprise. Everyone contributes and everyone benefits. These are the values that will shape our season.

"If I had one message for the coming season, to everyone who cares about this amazing club, it is that we are ready for some great times if we are prepared to work together to achieve it."

With Mane starting on the substitutes' bench after just five days back with the squad, the Reds produced a dominant display under the glare of the Sky Sports cameras. They raced into a 4-0 half-time lead over Daniel Farke's visitors with an own-goal by defender Grant Hanley followed by strikes from Mohamed Salah, Van Dijk and Divock Origi. The Canaries pulled a goal back after the break through Finnish striker Teemu Pukki but Liverpudlians went home happy.

The only shadow over the victory was a calf injury sustained by keeper Alisson while taking a first-half goal-kick. The Brazilian, replaced by new signing Adrian to a rapturous Kop reception, seemed likely to be ruled out for several weeks.

"It was the start of the Premier League, we wanted to go out and start really well, which we managed to do," said captain Jordan Henderson of the team's opening night display.

"We scored some brilliant goals and played well in the first half. In the second half we created some chances but could have controlled the game a little bit better.

"There's still improvement [to be made] but overall we're delighted with the result and performance."

Onto the next Premier League game? Not quite yet. As European champions the Reds had the chance to add another UEFA Super Cup to their roll of honour and headed out to Istanbul in midweek to take on Europa League winners Chelsea in the showpiece fixture.

In front of a partisan crowd of Reds seemingly from all over the region, Liverpool emerged victorious in a penalty shoot-out following a 2-2 draw in 120 minutes.

Mane, back in the starting line-up and looking sharp as ever, cancelled out Oliver Giroud's opener to take the game to extra-time. The Senegalese then put the Reds ahead when he beat Blues keeper Kepa Arrizabalaga with a stunning finish. Chelsea levelled from the spot when Tammy Abraham went to ground as he contested a loose ball with Adrian. VAR [Video Assistant Referee] saw the decision stand and Jorginho equalised from 12 yards.

In the subsequent shoot-out Adrian was Liverpool's hero, saving the 10th and final kick from Abraham to give the Reds a 5-4 victory and secure the trophy for the fourth time.

It was Liverpool's 46th major honour, taking them one clear of Manchester United in the trophy count. During the celebrations that followed, Klopp channelled his inner Sylvester Stallone for the camera by shouting "Adriannnnn!" like the *Rocky* movies.

"It was my first game in the starting eleven so I had to prepare mentally as everything had happened so quickly," the keeper admitted.

"I am delighted that very quickly I have helped to write the next stage in the history of the club and I wanted to have a hand in that. Of course it was not only my hands but my right foot at the end to save that penalty!

"When you are winning this kind of title it gives you more confidence to keep playing in the league too. It can give us a great boost and now we are more than ready to keep playing."

Daily Telegraph journalist Jason Burt claimed that the shoot-out triumph could provide a telling psychological boost in a season which would likely entail north of 55 games: "Try telling Liverpool the Super Cup does not matter.

"Try telling Jürgen Klopp who sprinted to wrap his arms around Adrian. Try telling the second-choice goalkeeper, without a club a few days ago, who made the crucial save in the shoot-out and later cherished the trophy to make himself an instant Anfield hero. And try telling Liverpool's fans and their co-owner John W Henry who tweeted one word: 'Beautiful'.

"Winning is a habit and Liverpool have their second European trophy in a few short months, and while it felt a little mad that extra-time was played, that players were dropping to the turf with cramp and others folded in exhaustion in 24-degree heat beyond midnight, there was simply no relenting, no inch given.

"It was a quarter to one in the morning in Istanbul when Chelsea substitute Tammy Abraham stepped up to take the tenth spot-kick in the shoot with all the previous nine having been converted. Adrian saved with his legs and the celebrations exploded, compounded by the fact that nine-tenths, if not more, of the stadium was decked in red. Such is Liverpool's global reach."

Adrian was quickly brought down to earth – literally – by needing a late fitness test to play in the next Premier League game at Southampton. He'd picked up an ankle injury after colliding with an over-exuberant fan who ran onto the pitch amid the celebrations that followed that Super Cup triumph in Istanbul.

The day before the Southampton game, news broke that young local talent Curtis Jones had signed a long-term contract with the club – he would of course reappear later in this story – while soon after England man Alex Oxlade-Chamberlain followed suit.

Down on the South Coast meanwhile goals from Mane and Firmino at St Mary's helped the Reds secure a 2-1 win, with the Senegalese ace becoming the first player to score in his first Premier League start of a campaign in four back-to-back seasons since Mark Viduka between 2002/03 and 2005/06.

The victory did not come without a few late scares. A patched-up Adrian saw his injury manifest itself in the 83rd minute when he cleared the ball against the shin of substitute Danny Ings to gift the Saints striker a goal against his former club. In a dramatic finale Ings then squandered a great chance to equalise

"Adrian had a swollen ankle and we played too many balls back to him in that period," conceded Klopp. "The other players have to then feel more the responsibility for the build-up and cannot give all the balls back to him

"I AM DELIGHTED THAT VERY QUICKLY I HAVE HELPED TO WRITE THE NEXT STAGE IN THE HISTORY OF THE CLUB"

and hope the pain-killers still help or whatever."

Nonetheless the victory saw Klopp amass 300 league points in fewer games than any manager in the club's history. It was the German's 146th league fixture in charge since he took over in October 2015, surpassing the 150-mark previously set by Kenny Dalglish.

Later that Saturday evening, as Kopites would duly have noted, reigning champions Manchester City drew 2-2 at home to Tottenham, ending their own 15-match winning streak in the Premier League.

The following midweek, midfielder Alex Oxlade-Chamberlain gave supporters more reasons to be cheerful when he committed to a new long-term contract with the club.

The England man was realistic but defiant in his outlook: "We've had a taste of winning [a trophy] and we knew what it took to get there. It was nowhere near easy.

"I think it's going to get harder and harder. We know what it's going to take. There are going to be moments that test us and maybe new tests this year that we didn't face last year.

"We had to dig in [at Southampton, for example]. The boys dug in all last year through difficult moments, where you're expected to win and still go out and win. We know there's going to be tests and we know that's what's required."

Next up was a visit from Unai Emery's Arsenal and the Reds produced a fine display to beat the Gunners 3-1 and remain the only team in the top four divisions with a 100 per cent winning start.

Joel Matip power-headed the opening goal – his first for Liverpool at the Kop-end – before a second-half brace from the lethal Salah wrapped up an impressive victory.

"It was a performance full of power, energy, greed and passion, which I think you need against a team like Arsenal," a delighted Klopp told Sky Sports. "The last ten minutes I saw the possession – 53 to 47 per cent or something like that – but over 80 minutes it must have been completely different. We were completely in charge of the game."

Before the first international break of the season, the Reds faced the short journey to Lancashire neighbours Burnley.

There was more good news ahead of the trip to Turf Moor as Alisson was named as the UEFA Champions

League goalkeeper of the season for 2018/19 and Van Dijk as the UEFA Champions League defender of the season for 2018/19.

Van Dijk was also crowned UEFA's Men's player of the year for 2018/19.

The Liverpool defender's outstanding form for club and country saw him beat Lionel Messi and Cristiano Ronaldo to the prize but he was quick to pay tribute to his LFC colleagues: "First of all, I need to thank all of my team-mates. Without all of them and without the staff, I wouldn't have achieved what I've achieved over the last year especially.

"I thank my family, of course. It's been a long road but that's part of my journey. It's part of who I am. I needed it like this – I'm not a player who was 18 years old and had that rise straightaway. I had to work hard for every step of the way – that's part of me and I'm very happy about that.

"I'm very proud to get this trophy and it's all credit to everyone that's helped me along the way."

An encouraging first month finished with a comprehensive 3-0 win at Burnley which also set a new club record of 13 straight league victories.

Trent Alexander-Arnold's cross deflected off Clarets striker Chris Wood and up and over keeper Nick Pope for the opener 12 minutes before half-time. It was quickly followed by a Mane goal before Liverpool clinched the three points after the break as Firmino became the first Brazilian in Premier League history to score 50 goals.

Another good stat was that Liverpool became only the second English top-flight side to win 13 games in a row while scoring more than once each time (after Tottenham in 1960), causing *Guardian* journalist Paul Wilson to remark: "Jürgen Klopp and his players really are writing themselves into the club's history books, since not even the great sides assembled by Shankly, Paisley or Dalglish ever managed that.

"Impressive as the achievement is, however, there is no doubt that fortune favoured the visitors in the first half. Burnley gave a good account of themselves for half-an-hour until the complexion of the game was altered by two Liverpool goals in quick succession, the first a ludicrous own goal and the second a defensive gift.

"Liverpool will not mind. Their only priority at the moment is staying ahead of Manchester City for as long as possible and they can now spend the international

break looking forward to Newcastle at home when the domestic programme resumes.

"Burnley may not have been expecting to win this game anyway, though having its outcome established so early meant they were obliged to spend most of the second half watching their opponents stroke the ball around."

Captain Henderson said of the display: "I thought we did the 'dirty bits' really well.

"We worked extremely hard defensively to win second-balls, which is important against Burnley. The two strikers [Chris Wood and Ashley Barnes] are really physical. I thought we coped with them really well.

"Going forward we looked good at times and scored some brilliant goals. It was a really good performance."

Plenty of positives to draw on then as Reds stars, replete with four league wins out of four and another European trophy in the bag, jetted off around the globe for the first international engagements of the new campaign.

UEFA Super Cup winners:
Liverpool FC

Barclays Premier League
manager of the month:
Jürgen Klopp

UEFA Champions League
goalkeeper of the season
for 2018/19:
Alisson Becker

UEFA Champions League
defender of the season
for 2018/19:
Virgil van Dijk

UEFA's Men's player of the
year for 2018/19:
Virgil van Dijk

STANDARD CHARTERED PLAYER OF THE MONTH FOR AUGUST:

Mohamed Salah

Mo was voted Liverpool's star man in August after three goals and two assists in six appearances in all competitions, edging out fellow forwards Roberto Firmino and Sadio Mane in this poll on the club's official website.

"I am happy to win the award but the most important thing as I've said before is winning games," insisted Salah. "We had a good month, we won a trophy in that time [and] everyone showed with our performances the way we can play, so we're happy about what we have right now."

AUGUST GOAL OF THE MONTH:

Mohamed Salah v Arsenal

Mo netted twice against the Gunners at Anfield, his second a clinical finish after surging beyond David Luiz near the halfway line and racing clear to score. Sadio Mane's emphatic curler in the 2-1 win at Southampton came second, while Salah's side-footed effort against Norwich in the season-opener was third.

PREMIER LEAGUE TABLE 01/09/2019

	P	W	D	L	F	A	GD	Pts
Liverpool	4	4	0	0	12	3	9	12
Manchester City	4	3	1	0	14	3	11	10
Leicester City	4	2	2	0	6	3	3	8
Crystal Palace	4	2	1	1	3	2	1	7
Arsenal	4	2	1	1	6	6	0	7
Everton	4	2	1	1	4	4	0	7
West Ham	4	2	1	1	6	7	-1	7
Manchester United	4	1	2	1	7	4	3	5
Tottenham	4	1	2	1	7	6	1	5
Sheffield United	4	1	2	1	5	5	0	5
Chelsea	4	1	2	1	6	9	-3	5
Burnley	4	1	1	2	5	6	-1	4
Southampton	4	1	1	2	4	6	-2	4
Newcastle	4	1	1	2	3	5	-2	4
Bournemouth	4	1	1	2	5	8	-3	4
Brighton	4	1	1	2	4	7	-3	4
Wolves	4	0	3	1	4	5	-1	3
Aston Villa	4	1	0	3	4	6	-2	3
Norwich City	4	1	0	3	6	10	-4	3
Watford	4	0	1	3	2	8	-6	1

2

BIG AWAY WINS AND THE START OF
THE CHAMPIONS LEAGUE DEFENCE

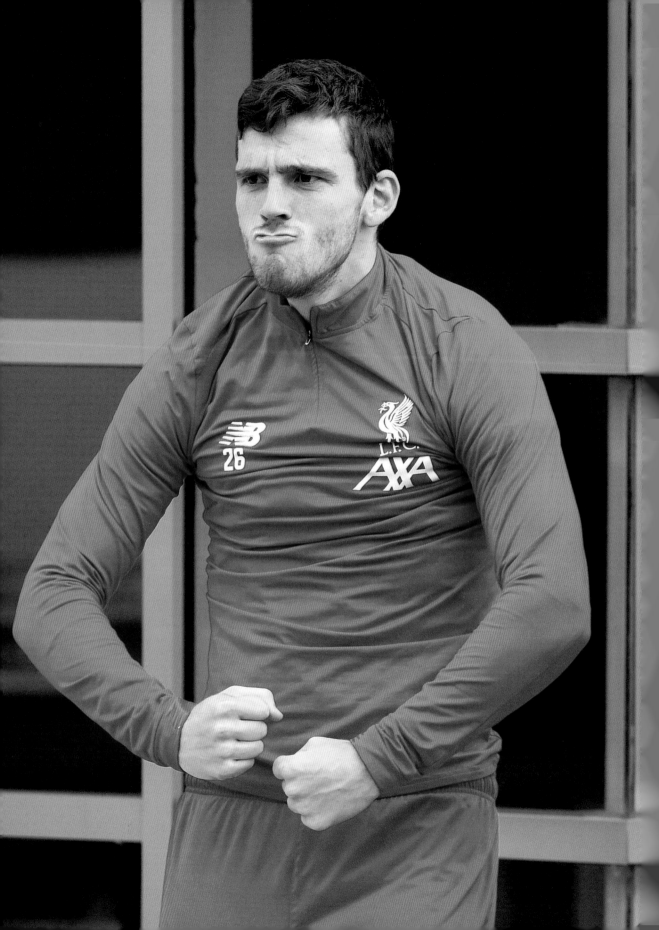

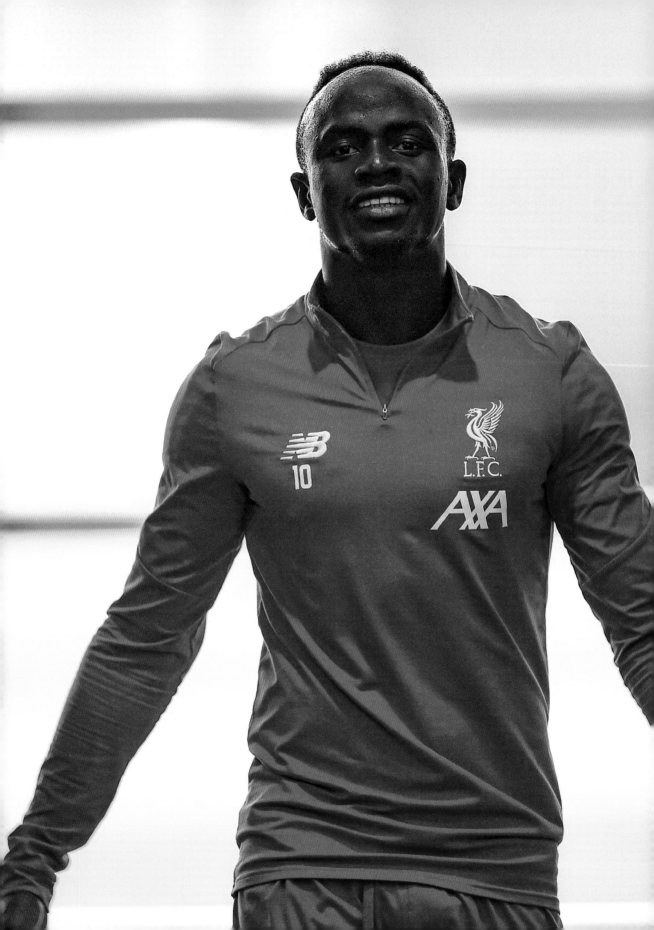

The morning before Jürgen Klopp addressed the media at Melwood ahead of the Reds' return to Premier League action, the boss received some pleasing news.

Friday the Thirteenth of September proved to be lucky for Klopp as he was named Premier League manager of the month for August. Overseeing his team's 100 per cent start to the league campaign, he held off competition from fellow nominees Pep Guardiola (Manchester City), Roy Hodgson (Crystal Palace) and Brendan Rodgers (Leicester City) to win the accolade.

His main focus now, however, was on making sure his players were sufficiently recovered from their various international flights to carry on where they left off. Newcastle United were their opponents at Anfield at half-past-noon on Saturday before the Liverpool squad flew to Italy to begin their defence of the Champions League in Naples.

The Reds were given an early fright against the Magpies when visiting left-back Jetro Willems scored a stunning opener at the Anfield Road end. But the hosts fought back with two goals from Sadio Mane putting them ahead at the break.

Victory was complete when Mo Salah rounded off a wonderful team-goal with a brilliantly deft assist from fellow forward Roberto Firmino, who'd started the game on the bench after flying more than 10,000 miles to fulfil his duties with Brazil.

Klopp later admitted that he was so impressed with Bobby's performance that he considered joining in the Kop's *Si Senor!* song which paid homage to the Brazilian. "I was close to singing it!"

"It was really good [from him today]. We knew that he could play. It's not about that – it's just the trip that he had. They [Firmino and fellow Brazil international Fabinho] were in Miami and LA and arrived on Thursday morning after playing Tuesday night. It's really difficult to judge these situations and that's why we made the decision.

"It was the right decision and we had changed in the game already because Div [Origi] was a bit too wide,

Mo was a bit too wide. Sadio, he can play that [central] position as good as anybody, but we decided to change because we wanted Sad a bit more flexible and coming from the wing inside.

"Then Div unfortunately showed that he could not carry on [and was replaced by Firmino on 37 minutes]. But of course what Bobby did then on the pitch – phenomenal. Nice game!"

Trent Alexander-Arnold also paid tribute to his team-mate: "You'd struggle to name a better link-player. If you're talking about the Premier League I think Bobby is the best and he is still so underrated for what he does for the team.

"Maybe the two other forwards, Sadio and Mo, get all the credit for their goals, but what Bobby does for them can go unnoticed. He drags defenders out of positions so they can get in behind them and the way that he presses and wins the ball back is relentless. He's exactly what we need."

The Newcastle win made it five out of five for Liverpool as far as the Premier League was concerned but the Champions League campaign got off to a sticky start with a 2-0 defeat at Napoli. The Serie A side went ahead from the penalty-spot after Andy Robertson was adjudged to have fouled Spanish attacker Jose Callejon and VAR allowed the decision to stand despite there seeming to be little contact. Attacking midfielder Dries Mertens converted the spot-kick before striker

Fernando Llorente added a late second as the holders chased an equaliser.

Virgil van Dijk said afterwards that the Reds should enjoy their status as European champions even though it made them a key scalp for opposing teams: "I think everyone wants to beat us no matter what competition.

"That's something we have to deal with, but it's not going to be a problem at all.

"We have to enjoy that. For us to lose our first game is obviously not what we wanted, but the only thing we can do is try to win all the other games and now focus on the next game at Chelsea."

Ahead of the trip to Stamford Bridge, full-back Alexander-Arnold revealed he wanted to add more goals to his game: "It's something I'd like to improve. The modern-day full-back needs to be so attacking, needs to offer a lot to the side, whether that be chances created, assists, passes, through-balls.

"I THINK EVERYBODY WANTS TO BEAT US, NO MATTER WHAT COMPETITION, BUT IT'S NOT A PROBLEM"

"Why not take it a step further and add four or five goals in to help the team?"

Trent's words prove prophetic as he opened the scoring in the excellent 2-1 win at Chelsea, lashing home from a free-kick before fellow full-back Andy Robertson picked out Firmino to head home from another set-play.

Chelsea pulled a goal back after the break through midfielder N'Golo Kante but the Reds held on to make it six wins out of six in the Premier League and 15 on the bounce dating back to the previous season.

Meanwhile Klopp received another personal accolade when he was named as the Best FIFA men's coach for 2019. He accepted the award at a ceremony in Milan, topping a ballot of national-team captains, coaches, fans and football journalists.

There was no let-up in the hectic schedule as Liverpool headed south to play their first Carabao Cup tie of the season in their first-ever meeting with MK Dons.

There were several new faces as the Reds won 2-0 to book a fourth-round date with Arsenal at Anfield. Goals from full-backs James Milner and Ki-Jana Hoever were enough for Liverpool to prevail in front of an MK Dons record crowd of 28,521.

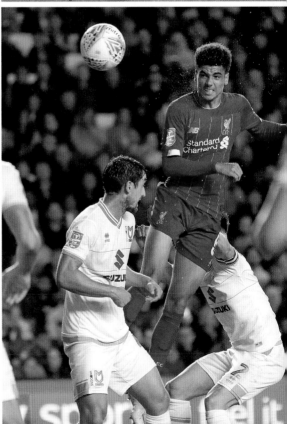

Jürgen Klopp gave full first-team debuts to goalkeeper Caoimhin Kelleher, forward Rhian Brewster and attacking midfielder Harvey Elliott. Centre-back Sepp van den Berg and midfielder Herbie Kane made their own debuts off the bench.

Back in the league the next assignment was a tough-looking trip to Sheffield United. The promoted Blades had made an impressive start to the season under manager Chris Wilder and Liverpool knew they will be given a stern test at Bramall Lane.

They came through it with a 1-0 victory, although only after a slice of luck. Gini Wijnaldum scored the second-half winner for Liverpool, playing in their third kit of 'phantom black and vibrant Tidepool', his shot squirming through the fingers and legs of the otherwise-excellent Blades goalkeeper Dean Henderson.

"If it was a draw, I would have been sat here saying that is what we deserved," Klopp reflected at his post-match press-conference. "Winning on the cloudy days is valuable for sure. We weren't at our best – they made it incredibly hard."

Wijnaldum stressed the importance of finding a way to win as he analysed the team's early-season displays: "So far this season we have played a few teams who have tried to win the game and a few of them who have also dropped deep and tried not to concede a goal or lose the game. The good thing for us is that so far we have found a way to win.

"We have made progression as a team over the years with the games we have played and the experience we

have gained from them. Maybe a few years ago we might have drawn that game or lost it, but because that happened in the past we have learned from it and managed to take it to where we are right now."

The win in South Yorkshire made it seven out of seven in the Premier League and the Reds were the first team to achieve that feat since Chelsea in 2005/06. Klopp's side also had the record books rewritten as Bramall Lane became the 56th ground at which Liverpool had won in the Premier League era – four more than any other side.

Champions League football returned to Anfield at the start of October in what was Liverpool's 100th European fixture at their famous home, and ahead of the clash with FC Salzburg they made a key addition to their coaching staff. Vitor Matos joined as elite development coach, having previously served as assistant-coach of FC Porto's B-team which played in the Portuguese second tier.

The 31-year-old took up the position previously held by current Reds assistant-manager Pepijn Lijnders, who'd also made the switch to Merseyside from Porto.

Sadio Mane had extra reason to look forward to the Champions League night, having made his name in Europe with FC Salzburg. At a pre-match press conference the forward said: "Of course it's a special game for me. I was playing there for two-and-a-half years and now I'm going to play against them.

"They will be ready for me and I will be ready for them as well. I love the city and the club – before and still now. I will be really happy to meet my ex-team-mates. But at the same time, I would love to win against them."

Klopp was wary of the threat posed by his team's Austrian opponents: "The way Salzburg plays is made for surprises for bigger teams."

The game itself was a thriller with Liverpool ultimately emerging as 4-3 victors but not without a scare or two. They raced into a 3-0 lead with goals from Mane, Robertson and Salah and appeared to be well in control.

But Salzburg cast off their nerves after the break and astonishingly were level at 3-3 by the hour-mark with Japanese international Takumi Minamino among their scorers. It needed a calm finish from Salah in front of the Kop to give the Reds the three points and get them up-and-running in Group E.

Before Liverpool signed off for the second international break of the season, they'd host another team who'd made a strong start to the campaign, Leicester City,

"I WILL ALWAYS BE GRATEFUL TO SIR KENNY DALGLISH FOR HAVING ENOUGH BELIEF IN MYSELF TO BRING ME HERE IN THE FIRST PLACE. BUT AS WELL AS SIR KENNY, BRENDAN PLAYED A MASSIVE PART IN MY LIVERPOOL CAREER AND DEVELOPMENT AS A PLAYER HERE" on Saturday 5 October. The game would see Brendan Rodgers return to Anfield for the first time since his departure in October 2015.

In his notes for the fixture in the matchday programme, captain Jordan Henderson wrote of his personal gratitude to Rodgers: "There is little room for sentiment in football and today I have no doubt at all that the manager in the away dugout will have as much desire to win here as we all have in looking to beat his side.

"That said, it's impossible to ignore the person, along with key staff members, returning to Anfield this afternoon for first time since they left Liverpool. For 90-plus minutes we are opponents, but the only way to describe Brendan Rodgers, Kolo Toure, Chris Davies and Glen Driscoll is as returning friends – and as people who did a lot to help not just this club as a whole but a number of individual players within it, myself included. I know they'll get a warm welcome before and after the game.

"I will always be grateful to Sir Kenny Dalglish for having enough belief in myself to bring me here in the first place. But as well as Sir Kenny, Brendan played a massive part in my Liverpool career and development as a player here."

The match was another entertaining affair with Liverpool leaving it until stoppage-time to maintain their 100 per cent winning start to their league season.

Mane opened the scoring with his 50th Premier League goal for the Reds in his 100th game, keeping his cool to beat goalkeeper Kasper Schmeichel in front of the Kop.

However, Leicester drew level after the break with James Maddison on target. Honours even? Not quite. The game was in added-time when Mane was brought down by winger Marc Albrighton and, following a VAR check, a penalty was awarded.

James Milner stepped up and was the coolest man inside Anfield as he swept home from 12 yards to give the Reds another vital three points.

Afterwards the vice-captain revealed his emotions as he waited for the VAR officials to make their ruling. "It was tough. There was a bit of a wait and I was just trying to concentrate on what I was going to do.

"The first thing was whether it was going to be given or not. That's obviously a new experience because

normally it's a penalty or it's not. So that was different, but I was just trying to stay calm.

"We're just delighted to get the win. It was always going to be tough, they're a good team. We looked pretty tired in the second half but we found a way to win again. It shows the character of the squad."

Milner's experience was key in the Reds' superb start and another man taking the plaudits was centre-back Joel Matip, certainly not one for taking the limelight.

His performances, though, alongside Van Dijk in the heart of defence caught the eye and he was subsequently named as the PFA Premier League player of the month for September.

In winning the award he saw off competition from Pierre-Emerick Aubameyang (Arsenal), Callum Wilson (Bournemouth), Ricardo Pereira (Leicester City) as well as Manchester City duo Kevin De Bruyne and Riyad Mahrez.

Alongside him, Van Dijk continued to exude an air of calm. Asked if he ever got nervous, the big no4 replied: "It's not nervousness any more, it's more excitement. I think that's the better word.

"A fear of failure is the worst thing you can have because you're going to make mistakes if you have a feeling that you can't make mistakes.

"But the thing is you need to look forward to going out there and showing your qualities. Show your qualities to the world but just enjoy it because before you know it, it's all over and I don't want to have any regrets at the end of my career that I should have done this, I should have done that.

"I just want to enjoy it. The only influence we have as players is on the pitch and with your team."

It was eight wins out of eight for this Reds team and an eight-point advantage at the top of the Premier League too for Van Dijk after Manchester City slipped to a 2-0 home defeat at the hands of Wolverhampton Wanderers the following day.

"I think if you look at our group, we have a pretty good squad," added the Dutchman. "Last year we were a bit unlucky with some injuries to certain players so hopefully we can all stay fit because we need everyone.

"Obviously the teams around us are trying to improve because they want to get as close as possible to Man City and ourselves after last year. But if I'm looking at our team and what we have right now, then we have a fantastic group and I believe we can go all the way."

SEPTEMBER AWARDS

PFA Premier League player of the month: **Joel Matip**

Best FIFA men's coach 2019: **Jürgen Klopp**

Best FIFA men's goalkeeper 2019: **Alisson Becker**

FIFA FIFPro men's world XI team 2019: **Alisson Becker and Virgil van Dijk**

STANDARD CHARTERED PLAYER OF THE MONTH FOR SEPTEMBER:

Roberto Firmino

Bobby got the vote after helping his side maintain their 100 per cent start to the Premier League season. "It's been another incredible month," he said.

"We played well, we've won games. I'm very happy with my development here at the club. My objective is to be constantly growing and contributing with goals and assists. With the quality that we have, we still haven't seen anything. We're maintaining our focus and we'll see how it goes."

SEPTEMBER GOAL OF THE MONTH:

Mohamed Salah v Newcastle United

Mo's goal in the 3-1 victory over the Magpies won Liverpool FC's September goal of the month award, with an honourable mention for the turn and flick from Roberto Firmino which made it possible. Trent's thunder-free-kick at Chelsea claimed second spot in the poll.

PREMIER LEAGUE TABLE 06/10/2019

	P	W	D	L	F	A	GD	Pts
Liverpool	**8**	**8**	**0**	**0**	**20**	**6**	**14**	**24**
Manchester City	8	5	1	2	27	9	18	16
Arsenal	8	4	3	1	13	11	2	15
Leicester City	8	4	2	2	14	7	7	14
Chelsea	8	4	2	2	18	14	4	14
Crystal Palace	8	4	2	2	8	8	0	14
Burnley	8	3	3	2	11	9	2	12
West Ham	8	3	3	2	11	11	0	12
Tottenham	8	3	2	3	14	12	2	11
Bournemouth	8	3	2	3	13	13	0	11
Wolves	8	2	4	2	11	11	0	10
Manchester United	8	2	3	3	9	8	1	9
Sheffield United	8	2	3	3	7	7	0	9
Brighton	8	2	3	3	8	10	-2	9
Newcastle	8	2	2	4	5	13	-8	8
Southampton	8	2	1	5	8	15	-7	7
Everton	8	2	1	5	6	13	-7	7
Norwich City	8	2	0	6	10	21	-11	6
Aston Villa	8	2	2	4	13	12	1	5
Watford	8	0	3	5	4	20	-16	3

STATEMENTS OF INTENT

3

DEFIANT AND UNDEFEATED
– WE SHALL NOT BE MOVED

I n mid-October 2019, as Liverpool FC's host of international stars returned from international duty around the globe, Jürgen Klopp and his coaches were preparing for a packed schedule of seven games in three competitions in three weeks.

The run through to the next international break would begin and end with Premier League fixtures against the Manchester clubs and there would also be a home date with Tottenham Hotspur, last season's Champions League final opponents, and a trip to newly-promoted Aston Villa.

Two days before the always-anticipated match against Manchester United at Old Trafford, the Reds received some positive news with centre-back Joel Matip signing a new long-term contract.

"It's a great feeling to be a longer part of the club," said the 28-year-old, who was now in his fourth season at Anfield.

"From outside you know Liverpool is such a big club, but when you are inside you really get a feeling for how big. The supporters are everywhere, in all countries. It's a massive club that every player would want to play for.

"We have a young and talented team and I think every one of us is hungry. Now we've seen how it is to win something and we want to have that feeling again.

There are a lot of things still to achieve. You never know how it will end, you just have to work hard and do the best you can. Then we will see."

Looking forwards was also in Klopp's mind when he was named Premier League manager of the month for a second time in the still-early season.

Ahead of the trip to Manchester, after being presented with the award at Melwood he said: "It's quite impressive what the boys did so far.

"There were moments when we needed a little bit of luck, that's clear — I don't forget Sheffield United and how we scored the goal there.

"But still, it's an impressive season so far from the boys and I'm their manager, so somebody thought: eight games in a row, we should give him the trophy for a second time. It's nice!"

Liverpool, without the injured Mohamed Salah, knew that Ole Gunnar Solskjaer's side, one point above the relegation zone at the time, would relish inflicting a first league defeat of the season on their fierce rivals.

It took a dramatic late equaliser from substitute Adam Lallana — in what would be his last season as a Red —

to earn a 1-1 draw at Old Trafford and keep the leaders unbeaten.

The game was not without controversy. Striker Marcus Rashford's opener for the hosts came after Divock Origi appeared to be fouled by United defender Victor Lindelof in the build-up, but a VAR check did not overrule referee Martin Atkinson's decision. Then Sadio Mane saw an 'equaliser' chalked off by VAR for handball.

Yet Liverpool kept pressing for a leveller in the closing stages while United dropped deeper and deeper to defend their lead.

Lallana, on for Jordan Henderson after 71 minutes, secured the point when he passed home Andy Robertson's low cross with five minutes remaining.

It was his first Premier League goal since May 2017 and afterwards he told Sky Sports: "We probably weren't

at our best today but sometimes you have to look to the bench and you have to come on and change the game.

"I thought Ox [Alex Oxlade-Chamberlain, replacing Origi on the hour-mark] did extremely well when he came on.

"If we're going to win the league and we're going to compete to take the title then we're not just going to need 11, we're going to need a squad. I think it is a point gained [as] we weren't at our best. Form goes out of the window in this type of game."

Another positive was the return of Alisson Becker in goal for the first time since picking up his calf injury during the opening-day win over Norwich City.

The following day he was named on a 10-man shortlist for the inaugural *France Football* Yachine Trophy for the best keeper in world football, an honour instituted as a goalkeeper-specific accompaniment to the annual Ballon d'Or.

Talking of which, Alisson and six other Liverpool players were named on the 30-strong list of nominees for that prestigious accolade. Joining the Brazilian goalie were Trent Alexander-Arnold, Roberto Firmino, Sadio Mane, Mohamed Salah, Virgil van Dijk and Georginio Wijnaldum. The winner would be announced at a ceremony in Paris on Monday 2 December.

"I am not sure who is not on the list from our boys!" quipped Klopp. "We have had so much attention and reward for the things that happened last year and that's all good. There is one more big day and then last season is closed.

"The boys deserved it. It is the big one and I am not

sure it happened too often that seven players from one club were on the shortlist and that's good. In the end someone will decide it. It's what the boys deserve for the season they played last year."

By now the Champions League was beckoning again and Liverpool claimed their second win in the group stages, 4-1 at Genk. There were two fine goals from Oxlade-Chamberlain, both from outside the penalty area, while Mane and Salah were also on target.

"It's a special tournament to play in, a competition we all grew up wanting to play in one day," Ox told BT Sport post-match. "It was nice to be back out there after seeing the boys do so well last year. I was fortunate enough to get back involved on the bench for the big day in the [2019] final and watch the boys bring it home.

"It's inspirational, something I've wanted to get back to do. It's just nice to be back in the starting line-up and try to put in a performance to help the team. To get a few goals was a bonus."

Liverpool's winning mentality was evident again when Tottenham came to Anfield the following weekend, on Sunday 27 October. Despite the blow of falling behind to a goal from England captain Harry Kane after only 47 seconds, a reaction-header after a deflected shot hit the bar, the Reds rallied to claim an important 2-1 victory.

For a while Liverpool's attacking efforts were repelled by Spurs keeper Paulo Gazzaniga, who made no fewer than 12 saves, the most by a keeper in the Premier League since Manchester United's David de Gea made 14 against Arsenal in December 2017.

However the hosts finally equalised seven minutes into the second half when skipper Jordan Henderson's shot, executed with his 'weaker' left foot as the ball bounced high in front of him, evaded two defenders and found the far corner of the Tottenham inside-netting in front of the Kop.

With a quarter-of-an-hour left, Mane was fouled by Spurs full-back Serge Aurier and Salah drilled home the resulting spot-kick hard and low.

Fabinho's own man-of-the-match performance earned the midfielder a new nickname from Klopp: "'Dyson' [after the vacuum cleaner] in the centre was there for each ball defensively – what a game he played, unbelievable!"

Many of the regular senior side were given an evening off for the next engagement as Klopp made eleven changes to his starting line-up for the Carabao Cup fourth-round tie with Arsenal at Anfield.

Like Liverpool the Gunners fielded a young side and it turned out to be a remarkable evening's entertainment in L4, the Reds ultimately booking a place in the quarter-finals in a Kop-end shoot-out following a five-all draw!

An early own-goal from visiting defender Shkodran Mustafi put Liverpool in front but Arsenal fired back with a strike from midfielder Lucas Torreira and two from

up-and-coming ace Gabriel Martinelli to claim a 3-1 advantage.

James Milner pulled one back from the spot before the break when 16-year-old Harvey Elliott – who'd become the youngest player to represent LFC at home – was fouled by Martinelli.

The breathless end-to-end encounter continued in the second period with the Gunners restoring their two-goal advantage through defender Ainsley Maitland-Niles. But Oxlade-Chamberlain brought the Reds back to within a goal with a brilliant strike before Divock Origi struck an equally excellent equaliser after being picked out by teenage midfielder Curtis Jones.

Arsenal thought they'd won it again when attacker Joe Willock scored with a stunning long-range effort of his own. Then in the fourth minute of added-time, teenage debutant Neco Williams, the Reds' man of the match, whipped in a cross from the right and Origi volleyed home spectacularly to make it 5-5 and take the tie to penalties. Klopp's astonished smile was a picture.

Another Anfield debutant, Caoimhin Kelleher, saved Arsenal's fourth kick from Dani Ceballos with a fine stop low to his right, allowing local lad Jones to step up and convert the winner in front of the Kop and give Liverpool a 5-4 triumph in the shoot-out.

Klopp was full of praise for a team which had included five teenagers. "I'm not sure when was the last time I had so much fun in a football game, to be honest – I saw 19 goals! Actually before the game I said to Rhian Brewster I would buy a ticket for this game because I was really excited about the opportunity we could give to the boys."

The draw for the last eight was made the following morning on BBC Radio 2's breakfast show by presenter Zoe Ball and ex-Reds goalkeeper David James. They handed Liverpool an away-tie at Aston Villa with the game scheduled for the same midweek in December as Liverpool's FIFA Club World Cup semi-final in Qatar!

For the time being, though, the Reds had another visit to Villa Park uppermost in their minds as they went to the West Midlands in search of more Premier League points.

The game against Dean Smith's promoted side would provide a stern test of Liverpool's resolve. Ultimately it would be looked back upon as pivotal.

Villa took the lead after 21 minutes when John McGinn's free-kick was turned home at the back-post by fellow midfielder Mahmoud Trezeguet. After a lengthy VAR review the goal was allowed to stand.

The technology debate resurfaced when Liverpool thought they'd levelled, Mane's cross converted by Firmino. Again VAR was consulted and the official at their base in Stockley Park came to the conclusion it was offside. A Premier League statement later elaborated that Firmino had been offside by 'an armpit'.

It looked like Villa would hold on to inflict Liverpool's first league defeat of the season but the Reds responded like champions-elect. There were only three minutes of normal time remaining when Andy Robertson picked his moment to net his first goal of the season.

The Scotland skipper met an excellent Mane cross from the right with a leaping, bullet header that gave Villa goalkeeper Tom Heaton no chance. Liverpool were level. This time the officials all agreed.

The Reds were not quite done. Four minutes into stoppage time Trent Alexander-Arnold whipped in a low-ish corner that Mane met courageously at the near-post, guiding a header into the far-corner to kick off wild celebrations among Liverpool's players and their travelling fans.

Liverpool Echo correspondent Paul Gorst wrote that the victors had "simply mastered the art of great drama. This resourceful team which Jürgen Klopp has constructed these past four years just does not know when it is beaten.

"Yet again, victory was snatched away from the jaws of defeat as they responded to another extreme examination of their Premier League title credentials."

Mane's goal was the thirty-fifth 90th-minute winner scored by Liverpool in the Premier League, 10 more than any other side in the competition's history with five having come since the start of the 2018/19 season.

"I don't always believe we can win every game but I never give up," said Klopp. "We know we can do better but on days like this you just need to be ready to fight."

Aged 21 years and 26 days, Alexander-Arnold had made his 100th appearance in all competitions for Liverpool in the win at Villa , becoming the fourth-youngest player to do so for the Reds. Only Michael Owen, Raheem Sterling and Robbie Fowler had reached the figure at a younger age. Since Trent's debut in October 2016, only Firmino (36) and Salah (28) had provided more goalscoring assists for Liverpool than his 22.

"It was good to get the win and the 100th game obviously is a proud milestone for me personally," he said. "It's something I've always dreamed of, something me and my family are so proud of, and I'm happy that we got the three points."

With the season's third international break looming in mid-November, the Reds had two more games to look after.

Liverpool they would have to beat "the best team in the world." He continued: "I think it's a great moment for our club and all the players. It's a moment to enjoy – but to enjoy giving everything on the pitch and to play the best football possible. We play a big game against a big team, perhaps one time in our life a game like this on this pitch. It's important to play and give our all."

On Bonfire Night, with fireworks exploding overhead and smoke in the air, Genk performed admirably on the pitch but Liverpool moved to the top of Group E with a 2-1 victory.

Gini Wijnaldum put the Reds ahead but Genk skipper Mbwana Ally Samatta, who would join Aston Villa in the January window, stunned the Kop by heading home a corner at the near-post to equalise just before the break.

In the second half Oxlade-Chamberlain produced a fine winner with a shot on the turn but the Reds had to survive some late pressure with Alisson making a big save from Bryan Heynen to keep the lead intact.

Champions League business taken care of. Now there was a buzz of excitement in the build-up to the next Premier League fixture: Manchester City at Anfield.

First, the Champions League return with Genk at Anfield. The matchday programme, its larger format for the tournament a hit with fans, showcased the commemorative bronze Liver Bird sculptures presented to opposition clubs in Europe by Liverpool FC, plus the story of the giant Spion Kop-surfing flag belonging to Reds fan Frank Graceffa.

Visiting manager Felice Mazzu told his pre-match press-conference that if his side were to overcome

After the previous season's title race and the epic Champions League quarter-final ties of 2017/18, there was a growing sense that this was a rivalry for the age as Klopp and Pep Guardiola competed to come out on top. Nonetheless the Reds boss insisted it was far too early in the season to describe the game as a 'must-win'.

When asked by Sky Sports he replied: "I'm sorry, maybe there are other people who are smarter than I am and see it like this. I don't see it like this.

"For me, it's a 100 per cent want-to-win game, 100 per cent with all I have. 'Must win' I never understood because that doesn't change the chances."

The game took place on Remembrance Sunday, 10 November, with the traditional, impeccably-observed minute's silence before the action commenced.

After eleven games of the Premier League campaign the Reds held a six-point advantage over City and they knew that the Anfield factor could help stretch that to nine. Liverpool did exactly that as they produced another scintillating display to defeat City 3-1, but as expected they were pushed all the way.

There was a key moment early on when City claimed a handball against Alexander-Arnold. Referee Michael Oliver waved play on and the Reds broke downfield in a swift passage of play that led to Fabinho hammering them ahead with a breathtaking long-range strike at the Anfield Road end. One-nil Liverpool.

Seven minutes later it was two, and what a move that made it happen. Alexander-Arnold switched the play with a left-footed cross-field pass for fellow full-back

Robertson who surged forward and picked out Salah superbly at the far-post. The Egyptian king hardly broke stride as he headed back across goalkeeper Claudio Bravo into the net.

It was a goal that would draw comparison with Terry McDermott's header in the legendary 7-0 win over Tottenham in 1978.

A tactical change at half-time saw captain Henderson deployed in a wider role on the right and six minutes after the re-start he provided the perfect cross to pick out Mane who hurled himself through the air to head home Liverpool's third.

City pulled a goal back with 12 minutes remaining through midfielder Bernardo Silva, but the Reds saw out the game to take the spoils.

Guardian journalist David Hytner pointed out: "Liverpool briefly held a ten-point lead over City last December, although that was cut to seven the following day when Pep Guardiola's team won their game-in-hand. And so the nine-point advantage which this victory gave to Liverpool felt like new ground – hugely significant new ground.

"It remains early days in the title race but nine points in favour of a team that has lost only one league fixture in 18 months is quite a cushion.

"Jürgen Klopp said that nobody wanted to be top only in November and the real pressure was yet to come but this was a major statement of intent."

Klopp later spoke of his pride at his team's intensity against the defending champions: "If you want to win against Manchester City, which is really, really difficult for each team in the world, you cannot play the way they play because they are definitely the best in the way they play. It makes no sense.

"So we have to try to push through our way. But [it was] intense from the first second, you could sense it was really important for both teams. Both teams were ready to put a proper shift in and they did."

Midfielder Wijnaldum was pleased with the way the Reds prevailed after City made it 3-1: "We've had situations a couple of years before where we were maybe carried away by scorelines. But over the years we have learned so much with this group of players.

"We were talking with each other, saying that we had to stay focused and we had to do the same things and everything.

"With City you know that they are such a good team

that they can turn things around and so you have to be 100 per cent concentrated. We were still aware that it could change. We'd had a game a few years before against City at Anfield where we led 4-1 and they brought it back to 4-3. I think we've learnt a lot from the past and we stayed focused."

Fellow Dutchman Virgil van Dijk stressed that it was only another three points but added: "Of course it was a bit special because you are playing against the champions, your direct rival.

"We all know there are so many games left that so many things can happen between now and May. We are very happy with the position we are in, but we cannot take it for granted. We just have to keep going and take it game-by-game."

So with an eight-point advantage over second-placed Leicester City at the top of the table, the Redmen headed off for the final international break of 2019. They did so armed with 34 points from a possible 36 after those first dozen matches.

As if to underline that level of consistency, one incredible statistic doing the rounds following the win over City was that no other team in history had managed to have double the points of the fifth-placed team in the table (Sheffield United had 17) after 12 league games.

The next challenge for Klopp and his men would be to maintain those standards during a month which would also see them bidding to become kings of world club football for the first time.

OCTOBER AWARDS

Barclays Premier League
manager of the month:
Jürgen Klopp

STANDARD CHARTERED PLAYER OF THE MONTH FOR OCTOBER:

Alex Oxlade-Chamberlain

As well as the gong for best goal (left and below) the Ox was also voted Liverpool's star man for October by fans, seeing off competition from Fabinho and Sadio Mane.

"It was a really, really good month for me and a step in the right direction to where I want to get back to. That's the thing with football, in the space of a week or two, a lot can change for an individual or a team – and I've sort of had that with Genk, Arsenal and then Genk again, with a really good win away at Aston Villa for us between as well."

OCTOBER GOAL OF THE MONTH:

Alex Oxlade-Chamberlain v Genk

A sublime, outside-of-the-boot finish (left) for his second goal in the 4-1 Champions League victory in Belgium. In the fan poll on the official website it beat Ox's long-range strike and Divock Origi's stoppage-time bicycle-kick, both versus Arsenal in the Carabao Cup.

PREMIER LEAGUE TABLE 06/10/2019

	P	W	D	L	F	A	GD	Pts
Liverpool	**12**	**11**	**1**	**0**	**28**	**10**	**18**	**34**
Leicester City	12	8	2	2	29	8	21	26
Chelsea	12	8	2	2	27	17	10	26
Manchester City	12	8	1	3	35	13	22	25
Sheffield United	12	4	5	3	13	9	4	17
Arsenal	12	4	5	3	16	17	-1	17
Manchester United	12	4	4	4	16	12	4	16
Wolves	12	3	7	2	16	15	1	16
Bournemouth	12	4	4	4	15	15	0	16
Burnley	12	4	3	5	17	18	-1	15
Brighton	12	4	3	5	15	17	-2	15
Crystal Palace	12	4	3	5	10	16	-6	15
Newcastle	12	4	3	5	11	18	-7	15
Tottenham	12	3	5	4	18	17	1	14
Everton	12	4	2	6	13	18	-5	14
West Ham	12	3	4	5	14	20	-6	13
Aston Villa	12	3	2	7	17	20	-3	11
Watford	12	1	5	6	8	23	-15	8
Southampton	12	2	2	8	11	29	-18	8
Norwich City	12	2	1	9	11	28	-17	7

"PERFECT FOR EACH OTHER"

4

KLOPP COMMITS HIS FUTURE TO
ANFIELD AS THE REDS ROLL ON

The timing of the November international fixtures couldn't have been much worse. Instead of being able to build on the momentum of the win over Manchester City at home, Jürgen Klopp's players now jetted off around the world to represent their countries – always a nervy time for Liverpool supporters with long memories of players returning to Melwood with injuries they didn't previously have.

Alex Oxlade-Chamberlain created a small piece of history when he opened the scoring in England's 1,000th international match – a 7-0 Wembley win against Moldova that secured qualification for Euro 2020. The Ox also got one in a 4-0 victory in Kosovo and wasn't the only Red to score while away.

Naby Keita was on target for Guinea in a 2-2 Africa Cup of Nations draw with Mali, while three days after the Netherlands secured their own Euro 2020 qualification, Gini Wijnaldum took the captain's armband off the rested Virgil van Dijk and hit a hat-trick against Estonia.

Perhaps Liverpool have unearthed a future penalty-taker too. Neco Williams scored twice from the spot for Wales Under-19s against Russia and although he then missed one against Kosovo, he netted from the rebound.

On the subject of full-backs, Steven Gerrard took time out from managing Rangers to chat with the *Liverpool Echo* about Trent Alexander-Arnold and Andy Robertson.

"What we have in Trent and Robbo now, straightaway you would put them in the world-class bracket," he said. "The thing for Trent now is: can he maintain that consistency for as long as he can? Because he can go on and be whatever he wants to be.

"What I would say is he is already there and we, as Liverpool fans, are blessed to have these two full-backs in the position because they are absolutely flying. They are so important and key to how Liverpool play and I love watching them."

Another waxing lyrical was Roberto Firmino. "I am

never tired of praising Klopp," he said while away with Brazil. "He has so many good things on and off the pitch. We learn so much from him in every way and have been showing on the pitch that we can grow more and more each day."

Two sad stories emerged on Saturday 16 November. Former LFC captain Johnny Wheeler, who scored 23 goals in 177 games for the Reds between 1956 and 1961, passed away at the age of 91.

And it emerged that former defender Dominic Matteo, who made 155 appearances for Liverpool between 1993 and 2000, had been taken seriously ill. The 45-year-old, a regular pundit on LFCTV, required emergency surgery on a brain tumour. Thankfully he would go on to recover.

On the Sunday after those announcements, history was made again at Anfield with the first-ever women's Merseyside derby taking place at the ground, and a crowd of 23,500 watching the Reds edged out 1-0 by the Blues.

Ahead of the men's return to Premier League action at Crystal Palace, centre-half Dejan Lovren reflected on how he'd forced his way back into the manager's starting XI.

"During pre-season we had a good talk and one of the key words was patience. I am a player who wants to play and win with the team. I didn't have so many minutes last year. I've taken my chance and at the moment I am here."

Patience and perseverance were precisely what Liverpool duly showed at Selhurst Park to earn another 2-1 away win thanks to a late Roberto Firmino goal.

Mo Salah was only fit enough to sit on the bench. Sadio Mane and Robertson played with knocks picked up while away. Brazilian trio Bobby, Alisson and Fabinho arrived back from international duty in Abu Dhabi 48 hours before kick-off. Klopp had little time to prepare his team, yet still they won.

VAR intervened to rule out a James Tomkins opener, Lovren clearly fouled when trying to head clear, before

Mane opened the scoring early in the second half. The shot he struck, from Robertson's cross, bounced off both posts before crossing the goalline for his eighth strike against the Eagles.

Wilfried Zaha netted an 82nd-minute equaliser, sending the flag-waving Holmesdale Road fanatics into a frenzy, but their joy was short-lived. When Virgil van Dijk met Alexander-Arnold's corner in the area, a goalmouth scramble ensued until the ball landed at the feet of Firmino. He picked his spot like a lighthouse keeper finding the rocks with his lamp on a foggy November night, to give Liverpool another three points.

"Today I have no problem that we were not brilliant because in a game like this you just have to make sure you're ready to fight for the result and we were from the first minute," said Klopp. "Getting a result at Crystal Palace, you never take for granted. So it feels good."

It also meant Liverpool had extended their unbeaten league run to 30 games, one short of the existing club record, while never before had any top-flight side racked up 37 points from the first 39 available. No wonder Liverpool players were in contention for awards.

Salah, Mane and Keita were shortlisted for the CAF African player of the year while Van Dijk was in contention to win the Ballon d'Or, something his manager believed he deserved. "If you give [it] to the best player of this generation then you should give it always to Lionel Messi, that's how it is. But if you give it to the best player of last season, then it was Virgil van Dijk.

"I don't know exactly how it will work, but that is how I see it. The best player of all? That's Lionel. Best player of last season? That's Virgil."

Klopp himself was inducted into the League Managers Association's Hall of Fame alongside Pep Guardiola for 'historic achievements in football management to date'.

"I've been in England for four years and enjoyed each second," he said. "I saw all the names with their pictures and it's really impressive. I don't feel pride very often in my life but in this moment I'm really proud because it's just something really special."

Next up at Anfield was Champions League football and a visit from Napoli. A win would secure qualification for Liverpool. Anything less and the reigning European champions would have to avoid defeat in Salzburg on Matchday 6 to progress. A night of opportunity turned into a night of frustration, not least due to an untimely injury suffered by Fabinho.

Napoli's Hirving Lozano landed awkwardly on the Brazilian's ankle whose night was over in the 19th minute. Liverpool readjusted with Wijnaldum coming on, but Carlo Ancelotti's side took the lead through Dries Mertens. It took VAR three minutes to decide that he hadn't elbowed Van Dijk in the build-up, nor was he offside.

Spanish referee Carlos del Cerro Grande wasn't popular with the Anfield crowd and infuriated Klopp so much with one decision that the Liverpool manager was booked for remonstrating, his first yellow card here.

The 65th-minute equaliser evoked memories of Dortmund 2016. James Milner sent the ball in from the right, Lovren rose highest at the far-post to head home. It earned a 1-1 draw and preserved Klopp's unbeaten European record at Anfield.

"My problem right now is that Fabinho is injured, not Salzburg [coming up]," Klopp told the media. It was serious enough to rule the Brazilian out of action for two months. So much for the 'luck' some rivals and pundits had suggested was on Liverpool's side following the win at Palace, an issue Jordan Henderson tackled in his matchday programme notes.

"I've heard a lot in recent months about 'luck' playing a part in some of the wins we've managed this season," he wrote. "Of course luck plays a part in football – it always has done and always will. But my experiences have shown me that the more you put into something, the more you get out – that's the real story about our team at the moment.

"My personal view is that it is the professionalism of this squad and the dedication to what we are looking to achieve that delivers the so-called luck. Only hard work and the highest standards allow the sort of moments we enjoyed in London to happen. Without that, the so-called luck is completely irrelevant."

The next fixture, at home to Brighton & Hove Albion, was played the day before the 60th anniversary of Bill Shankly's appointment as Liverpool manager in late 1959. Fellow legendary boss Bob Paisley had also been honoured the preceding week, club sponsor Standard Chartered using smart technology to create a 'virtual' Bob interacting with current first-teamers and club legends in the dressing-room.

Within 48 hours of the Brighton game the 2019 Ballon d'Dor winner would be announced, so perhaps it was apt that Van Dijk proved to be the match-winner.

Like big Ron Yeats in Shankly's team back in the day, Van Dijk became the cornerstone of Klopp's

Anfield success story when he joined the club from Southampton in 2018. A colossus at the back, he's always a threat from set-pieces, as the Seagulls found to their cost.

The opening six minutes saw Kopites wave Hillsborough banners and chant 'Justice for the 96' following the 'not guilty' verdict in the David Duckenfield trial 48 hours earlier. Anfield then saw Van Dijk score twice in the space of six minutes, heading two Alexander-Arnold set-pieces into the Anfield Road net.

Visiting keeper Mat Ryan kept Brighton in the game with a save or three and then, with 12 minutes to play, Alisson became the first Liverpool goalie sent

off at Anfield for 20 years when he handled Leandro Trossard's shot outside the area.

Adrian came on for Oxlade-Chamberlain – the first time a substitute goalkeeper had ever been brought on twice in the same season for the Reds – but was still lining up his wall when a quickly-taken Lewis Dunk free-kick beat him. The goal stood.

Brighton sensed an opportunity but this Liverpool team is made of stern stuff. They held on like tigers for victory, the crowd roaring them over the line. Adrian made a couple of late saves to ensure a 2-1 victory for the ten men, equalling the club record of 31 league games unbeaten. "We are in a good position points-wise, but we know we can do maybe that extra 10 per cent still," said Virgil at full-time.

With Manchester City dropping points at Newcastle on the same day, the Redmen heading into December no less than eleven points clear at the top. Yet there was to be no Ballon d'Or for Van Dijk as *France Football*'s panel of international journalists voted him into second place behind Messi.

"You need to respect greatness," said the Dutch international captain at a glittering ceremony in Paris.

"I was close but there was just someone a little bit better. I'm very proud of what I achieved last year, with Liverpool and Holland.

"I never thought I would be up for a Ballon d'Or until I was actually nominated. It says a lot about how my

career has been, it has never been easy. I came late but I never gave up on my dreams. Where I am right now is something I'm very proud of. It makes me want to work even harder and hopefully be here next year again."

Mane (fourth), Salah (fifth) and Alisson (seventh) also finished in the top 10 with the latter receiving the first Yachine Trophy, named after legendary Soviet goalkeeper Lev Yashin.

"It is a great honour to be here with these great players, men and women," said Alisson as he held the award in the safest hands in football. "I just want to thank my family, my wife, who support me everywhere I go. To my parents – they are in Brazil, I think, watching me – and to God.

"I don't feel lucky – I feel blessed and grateful. I also want to say thank you to my team-mates, to all the Liverpool staff. Thank you very much."

While Van Dijk and Alisson were in the French capital, the capital of football was gearing up for the 234th Merseyside derby with news that a 235th encounter between Liverpool and Everton would follow in January 2020 after the sides were drawn together in the FA Cup third round, again at Anfield.

First, the Premier League encounter on Wednesday 4 December, and the Toffees would part company with manager Marco Silva after being hit for five here for the first time since 1965.

Klopp shuffled his pack, bringing Adam Lallana into midfield and both Xherdan Shaqiri and Divock Origi into his forward line. Origi had scored against Everton at Anfield in 2016, 2017 and 2018, so maybe it was inevitable that he would add 2019 to the list, taking just six minutes to open the scoring with a sweet finish.

Shaqiri then slid home his first goal of the season and although Michael Keane pulled one back, Origi was soon running onto Lovren's pass and lobbing Jordan Pickford to make it 3-1.

When Mane – who already had two assists to his name – and Richarlison exchanged goals in the last minute of the first half, it was the first time six goals had ever been scored in the opening 45 minutes of the derby.

The only goal of the second period came in stoppage-time, courtesy of Wijnaldum, as Liverpool made it a new club-record 32 matches without defeat – and 100 Premier League victories for Klopp from 159 games.

"All the goals were incredible, outstanding," said the boss. "Wonderful goals, sensational passes, super pieces of football. I loved it a lot!"

It proved to be a good week for Jürgen. After naming his 23-man squad for the FIFA Club World Cup in Qatar – Joel Matip and Fabinho the two notable absences through injury – he was announced as the winner of what was called the Great Coaching Moment of the Year award for 2019. It was, of course, Barcelona in the previous season's Champions League semi-final second leg.

"It is a huge honour to be recognised by UK Coaching for this award and I'd like to thank everyone who voted, especially our fans who played their part in what was an incredible performance and unforgettable night at Anfield back in May," he said.

"When you are a coach there is nothing more rewarding and powerful than seeing what can be achieved when everyone – the players, the coaching team and the fans – pull together. It was without doubt one of the proudest nights of my coaching career."

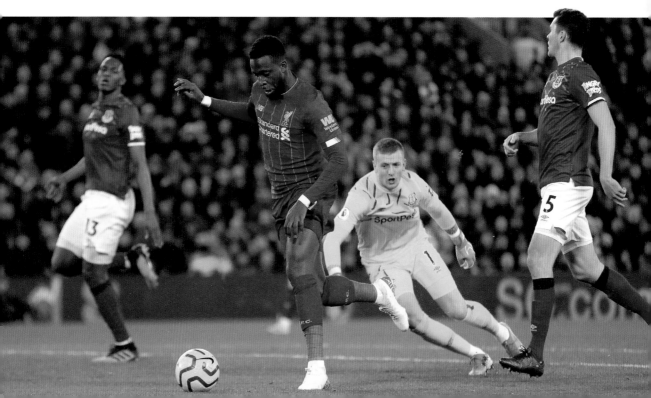

Liverpool had 21 shots on goal, Bournemouth had none. Alex Oxlade-Chamberlain got the first goal, nudging a volley past Aaron Ramsdale from Henderson's pass, before Salah came up with a contender for assist of the season when he back-heeled the ball past three defenders to tee up Naby Keita.

The two scorers were the 15th and 16th different players to net for LFC in the league in 2019/20, one short of the club record of 17.

Losing Lovren to injury was a blow, but Liverpool's third goal came when Keita repaid Salah for his assist by intercepting a stray pass and playing in the Egyptian to score his seventh goal against Bournemouth on his 100th Premier League appearance.

There was also a late Premier League debut for Curtis Jones and, later on that evening, a 2-1 home defeat for City in the Manchester derby. It left Liverpool 14 points clear of now third-placed City and never before, in the history of top-flight football in England, had a team won the league after finishing the day that far behind the leaders.

Alisson had kept Liverpool's first clean-sheet since September – a run of 13 games – at the Vitality Stadium. Incredibly it was also his first since the Champions League final against Spurs six months earlier. But it sparked a run of shut-outs in which he would only concede once in ten games, although he had to work hard to keep out RB Salzburg in Liverpool's must-not-lose Champions League group-stage finale in Austria three days later.

Saturday 7 December proved to be a vital day in the title race, albeit one of the less heralded perhaps due to the routine nature of Liverpool's 3-0 win at Bournemouth.

Since the 3-0 victory at Burnley in August, the Reds had won four of their five away matches by one goal and drawn the other 1-1 at Old Trafford. A drama-free away win was overdue and it came at the Vitality Stadium.

Teenage striker and wanted man Erling Haaland, scorer of 28 goals in 21 games, was leading the Salzburg line. Overall they'd scored an astonishing 94 times in their 25 matches in 2019/20, including those three at Anfield. They were brimming with confidence and came out of the starting-gate like a skier on the Alps.

Virgil van Dijk had to deal with threats from Haaland and Hwang Hee-chan in the opening 60 seconds before Alisson produced a brilliant double-stop to deny Hwang – teed up by Takumi Minamino's back-heel – and Minamino himself from the rebound.

Salah, Mane and Keita all saw opportunities come and go at the other end as a breathless opening half somehow finished goalless. Early in the second period Haaland crashed a shot into the side-netting before two goals in two minutes stunned the Austrian champions – Mane and Keita, two Salzburg old boys, coming back to haunt the Red Bull Arena.

Sadio chipped the ball over keeper Cican Stankovic for Keita to head home in the 57th minute, and the hosts were still reeling when Salah latched on to Jerome Onguene's weak back-header, took the ball past Stankovic and clipped home an eye-of-a-needle finish from the most acute of angles outside the area.

The sight of Haaland lashing a water bottle into the turf as Salah celebrated in front of the travelling Kop was telling. Liverpool were through as Group E winners and nine days later Minamino joined them after the Reds activated a release clause in his contract.

On Friday 13 December there was news for every supporter to get excited about. "Liverpool Football Club are delighted to announce Jürgen Klopp has agreed a contract extension with the club," read a statement on the official website. "The manager will extend his Reds tenure until 2024, ensuring he will remain at the helm for a further four-and-a-half years.

"Assistant-managers Peter Krawietz and Pepijn Lijnders have also agreed deals to continue working collaboratively alongside Klopp.

"The deal comes after four hugely successful years in charge of Liverpool for the 52-year-old and will ensure the long-term foundations for the team's – and indeed club's – development will continue well into the next decade."

With social media abuzz with the best early Christmas present imaginable, Klopp spoke about his decision to commit his future to LFC: "For me personally this is a statement of intent, one which is built on my knowledge of what we as a partnership have achieved so far and what is still there for us to achieve.

"When I see the development of the club and the collaborative work that continues to take place, I feel my contribution can only grow.

"People see what happens on the pitch as a measure of our progress and although it is the best measure, it's not the only measure. I have seen the commitment from ownership through to every aspect and function of the club you can think of.

"When the call came in autumn 2015 I felt we were perfect for each other. If anything, now I feel I underestimated that. It is only with a total belief that the collaboration remains totally complementary on both sides that I am able to make this commitment to 2024. If I didn't I would not be re-signing.

"This club is in such a good place, I couldn't contemplate leaving."

The news somewhat dwarfed the same-day announcement that Klopp had been named as Premier League manager of the month for the third time in the season, while Mane was selected as Premier League player of the month for November – an award Senegal's finest previously won in August 2017 and March 2019.

On paper Liverpool's next game, at home to Watford, looked like a nailed-on home win. The Reds were top on 46 points, the Hornets bottom on nine with only one win all season and new manager Nigel Pearson taking charge of his first game.

It proved to be a close encounter at a blustery Anfield.

Salah broke the deadlock in the 38th minute. Wijnaldum, Firmino and Mane combined to set him away as Liverpool counter-attacked from a Watford corner.

Kiko Femina dashed back to try to stop him, but the Egyptian cut back onto his right foot before brilliantly curling the ball beyond Ben Foster into the far-corner.

A minute before Salah's goal, and a minute after it, Abdoulaye Doucoure and Ismaila Sarr both mis-kicked in front of the Kop goal when presented with glorious opportunities to score. Big let-offs for Liverpool, although Watford were fortunate that VAR found an unspecified part of Mane's body offside when he headed home Shaqiri's cross to make it 2-0, it seemed, after the break.

Alisson made a couple of saves and Wijnaldum was forced off with a hamstring problem before Salah clinched all three points in the 90th minute. Origi miscued a shot from Mane's pull-back but Salah pounced to nutmeg Christian Kabasele on the goal-line with an audacious back-heel flick. Two very different goals, but they all count.

Mo's second meant that the Reds became the first team since Sunderland in 1891/92 – the season before Liverpool FC was formed – to win 16 consecutive top-flight games while scoring at least twice.

With second-placed Leicester being held at home by Norwich, the Reds headed off to Qatar for the FIFA Club World Cup with a ten-point lead at the top of the Premier League table.

Ahead of flying to Doha, it was pointed out to Klopp that Liverpool had never been world champions before. "I didn't think about that," he replied.

"I'm not someone who has to be the first on the moon or the first winning the World Cup with Liverpool, but when we are there then we will try with all we have."

And so they did.

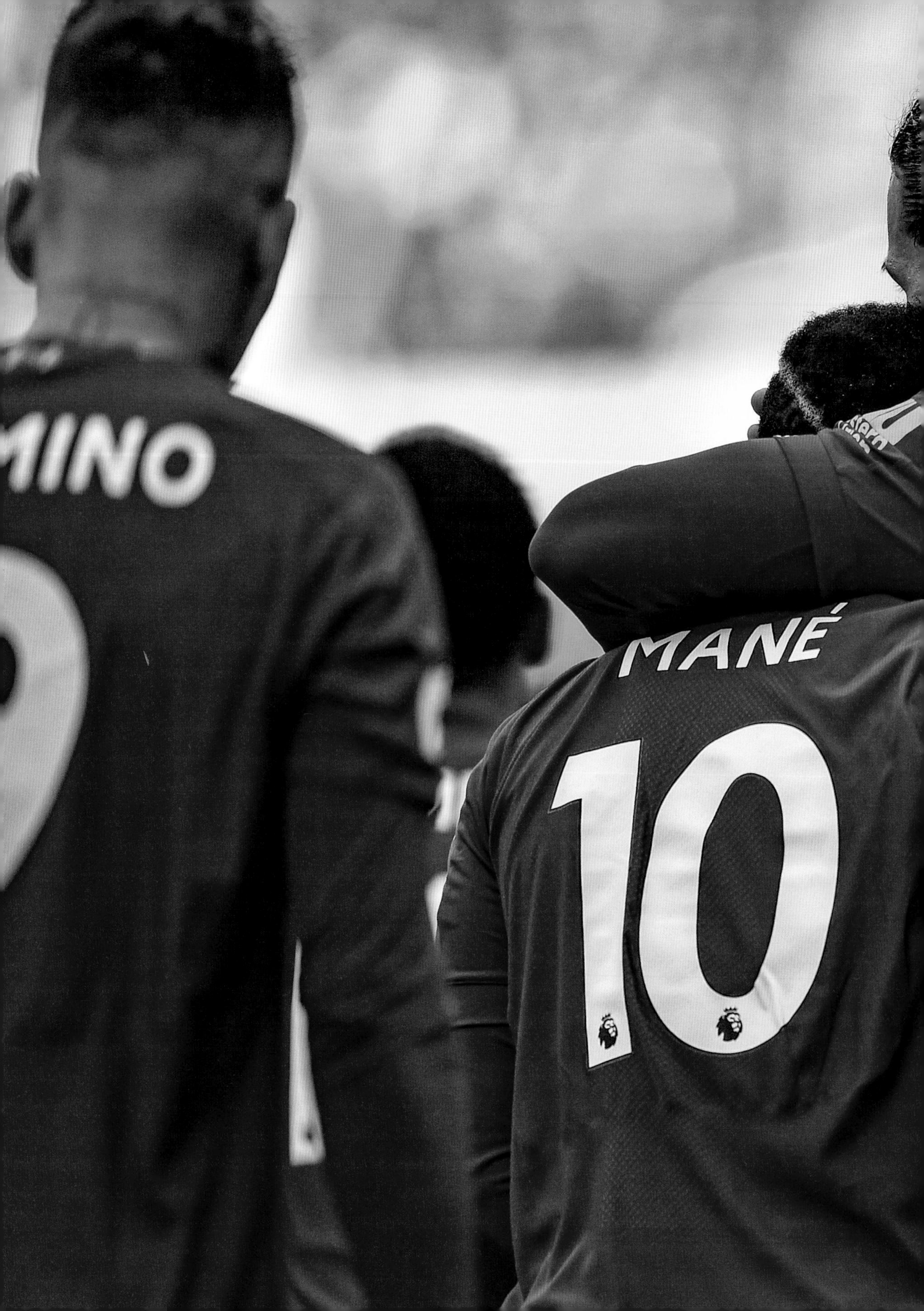
MINO
MANÉ
10

NOVEMBER AWARDS

Barclays Premier League
manager of the month:
Jürgen Klopp

EA Sports Premier League
player of the month:
Sadio Mane

League Managers
Association's Hall of Fame:
Jürgen Klopp

STANDARD CHARTERED PLAYER OF THE MONTH FOR NOVEMBER:

Sadio Mane

Three goals in five games was enough for Sadio to see of competition from Fabinho and Virgil.

NOVEMBER GOAL OF THE MONTH:

Fabinho v Manchester City

The Brazilian midfielder (left) opened the scoring in the 3-1 victory at Anfield by collecting a loose ball and rifling it home from 25 yards out. It topped the poll ahead of Mo Salah's header in the same game and Alex Oxlade-Chamberlain's turn-and-shot at home to Genk in the Champions League.

"For sure I am happy to win it and, like I always said, I'm here trying to be my best all the time. It has been a great few weeks for me and my team-mates so we just need to keep on going. I want to thank everyone who voted for me – big love for you guys!"

PREMIER LEAGUE TABLE 16/12/2020

	P	W	D	L	F	A	GD	Pts
Liverpool	**17**	**16**	**1**	**0**	**42**	**14**	**28**	**49**
Leicester City	17	12	3	2	40	11	29	39
Manchester City	17	11	2	4	47	19	28	35
Chelsea	17	9	2	6	31	25	6	29
Tottenham Hotspur	17	7	5	5	32	24	8	26
Manchester United	17	6	7	4	26	20	6	25
Sheffield United	17	6	7	4	21	16	5	25
Wolves	17	5	9	3	24	21	3	24
Crystal Palace	17	6	5	6	15	19	-4	23
Arsenal	17	5	7	5	24	27	-3	22
Newcastle United	17	6	4	7	17	24	-7	22
Burnley	17	6	3	8	22	29	-7	21
Brighton	17	5	5	7	21	25	-4	20
Bournemouth	17	5	4	8	19	24	-5	19
West Ham United	17	5	4	8	19	28	-9	19
Everton	17	5	3	9	20	29	-9	18
Aston Villa	17	4	3	10	23	30	-7	15
Southampton	17	4	3	10	18	36	-18	15
Norwich City	17	3	3	11	18	35	-17	12
Watford	17	1	6	10	9	32	-23	9

5

CUP HEROICS AT HOME AND
ALL-CONQUERING IN QATAR

Shortly after 7.45pm on a Tuesday night in mid-December, clusters of Liverpool supporters were gathered around smartphones, iPads and laptops in The Cabin Bar at Manchester Airport's Terminal 2.

There was a general hush as pint glasses were sipped from and eyes trained upon screens. These hardcore travelling Kopites were waiting to board an overnight flight to Doha – the last scheduled flight to leave T2 that evening – but their minds were in Birmingham.

The youngest Liverpool FC team in history were taking on a near full-strength Aston Villa side in the Carabao Cup quarter-final. Normally those intrepid Reds would have been at Villa Park in person, cheering Liverpool on, but this was no normal week.

Liverpool's participation in the FIFA Club World Cup, representing the UEFA federation as champions of Europe, caused a fixture clash with the Carabao Cup quarter-final. Unable to reschedule it to another date,

with the following weekend's Premier League fixture at West Ham United already postponed until February, it left Liverpool in an impossible position.

A decision had to be made and Jürgen Klopp made it. He opted to take his first-team to Qatar while putting faith in the club's youngsters to show their potential at Villa Park. It was a night when all kinds of records were broken.

Under-23s manager Neil Critchley stepped into Klopp's shoes and named the youngest starting line-up ever fielded by a Liverpool manager for a first-team game. An average age of 19 years, six months and three days was two years younger than any previous LFC XI.

Eight players made their debuts, the most in a single game since LFC's first fixture back in 1892. Morgan Boyes, Tony Gallacher, Isaac Christie-Davies, Thomas Hill and Luis Longstaff all started. Jack Bearne, Leighton Clarkson and James Norris came on from the bench.

Pedro Chirivella, a veteran at 22, wore the captain's

armband for the first time as the only member of the squad who had previously appeared in the Premier League for Liverpool.

Between them, Critchley's team had made a combined 16 appearances for LFC and in Harvey Elliott and Norris – the fourth-youngest player in the club's history – had two 16-year-olds on the pitch by full-time.

"One game like this is worth a million training sessions," said Critchley before kick-off. Despite his team losing 5-0, it was hard to disagree.

The scoreline, for the record Liverpool's heaviest defeat in the League Cup, didn't reflect the way the young Reds played against a strong Villa side. They gave a good account of themselves and gained the invaluable experience of playing against a Premier League side on live television for the European champions.

Elliott and Herbie Kane forced home goalkeeper Orjan Nyland into a couple of early saves, but when Conor Hourihane's 14th-minute opener was swiftly followed by a freak Boyes own-goal, the kids were up against it. A Jonathan Kodjia double made it 4-0 before half-time but only a stoppage-time goal from Wesley prevented a second-half clean-sheet for Caoimhin Kelleher.

"I thought we were magnificent," said Critchley at full-time. "We were fantastic from the start, we had a couple of chances from the first whistle. We were really unfortunate to concede and then found ourselves two-nil down.

"It was an incredible night and no-one wanted it to end. The support we had was unbelievable. The conduct of the Villa players was first-class. Dean Smith and John Terry came into our dressing-room after the game and said, 'keep going, good luck' and wished us the best. My overwhelming feeling is one of immense pride."

Klopp and his players watched the match in the marble-floored St Regis Hotel in Doha's West Bay, their Qatar base for the week. One young member of his squad was impressed with what he saw.

"It was always going to be difficult but I think the way that they played was outstanding – I felt proud watching them," said Trent Alexander-Arnold.

"It was almost a mirror-image of how the first-team play. The confidence, the courage, playing with a high line, the counter-press – it showed that the messages that are getting relayed back to the Academy are the same as those given to us at Melwood.

"The lads who went out there and gave such a good

account of themselves deserve a massive round of applause."

Qatar, bordered only by Saudi Arabia and surrounded by the Persian Gulf, is a country that has grown out of the desert thanks to the third-largest natural gas and oil reserves in the world and, as a result, the highest per capita income.

The 2022 FIFA World Cup will be held here, but extreme summer temperatures mean that, for the first time, the tournament will be staged in late November and December, forcing a six-week break in domestic football.

It made FIFA's 2019 Club World Cup, in effect, Doha's first 'test event' for the World Cup – and the travelling Kop were more than happy to be the guinea pigs if it meant seeing their team become world champions.

Netherlands. Germany. Czech Republic. Slovakia. Hungary. Romania. Bulgaria. Turkey. Iraq. Kuwait. Bahrain. The road to glory takes many different routes when you are a Red, but the Qatar Airways flight-path to Hamad International Airport was a little different than going down the M6 to Stoke on a wet Wednesday night.

A little over six hours after take-off, and with plenty of Reds having watched Christmas films en route to a new far foreign land, it was touchdown in Qatar. Eyes were scanned. Fingerprints were taken. Hotel details were noted. Passports were stamped.

The airport is a 15-minute ride from the centre of Doha in a taxi or on the pristine new Doha Metro which had only opened seven months earlier. The stop at the airport, appropriately on the red line, had only been in service for a couple of weeks and with a day pass

costing roughly £1.25 it was the choice of transport for many. It also happened to be National Qatar Day.

To mark the annual event, celebrated on 18 December to commemorate Qatar's unification in 1878, most nationals got the day off work and school. A huge parade, featuring government and military officials plus a fly-by and fireworks, took place on Doha's Corniche, the waterfront promenade that stretches for seven kilometres, with numerous road closures.

It was the biggest party of Doha's year and the Kopites who emerged from the Souq Waqif metro station were greeted by hundreds of flag-waving Qataris – many leaning out of car windows – with locals selling other memorabilia like the street sellers on the approaches to Anfield on a matchday.

Souq Waqif is a traditional Middle East market squeezed into narrow alleyways and backstreets, some of it indoor, some of it outside. Perfumes, garments, spices, jewellery, rugs, handicrafts, traditional dress, birds, puppies, souvenirs... If you can't find what you're looking to buy in Souq Waqif, it probably isn't for sale in Doha.

A wide variety of restaurants representing different nationalities – 2.3 million of Qatar's 2.6 million population are expatriates – and shisha bars line the streets. Persian, Syrian and Turkish establishments were plentiful, but alcohol was far more difficult to come by.

Dressing conservatively is the norm, although there was a relaxed attitude towards visiting football fans wearing shorts, preparing Qataris for the influx of so many different nationalities that a World Cup will bring with it.

The only public shows of affection that are permitted include greeting someone and celebrating a goal at a sporting event. Which was useful as the Redmen had more goals in them.

Liverpool played Mexico's CF Monterrey on Qatar National Day at the Khalifa International Stadium. The original venue for the semi-final, Education City – one of eight new or upgraded stadiums that will host the World Cup – hadn't been completed in time, forcing a late switch.

"We represent Europe, but we don't have the burden of Europe on our shoulders," said Klopp in the build-up. "We don't see ourselves as challengers because it will be the first time to win it. For us, we are here – we don't fly 3,000 miles not to show up."

Across the city at Doha Sports Park, next to Doha Golf Club, was Qatar's first-ever fan zone. It was a metro trip and shuttle bus ride away, off the beaten track and well away from the city-centre. That was because it was the first outdoor venue where beer, at £5-a-pint, had ever been served in Qatar and the location where many of the estimated 2,000 travelling Kopites congregated each night. They weren't just there for the food and drink, either.

From small beginnings in a 2011 post-match gig at the Static Gallery on Liverpool's Berry Street, BOSS Nights are now a Liverpool phenomenon. The fan zone in Qatar was organised by BOSS Night founding father Dan Nicholson and pre-match sets were played by Kieran Molyneux and Jamie Webster. The Lightning Seeds would later take to the stage the night before the final.

Webster and co got Liverpool's travelling contingent in the mood, belting out belter after belter, before shuttle buses were boarded and taxis hailed. All roads led to the Khalifa International Stadium.

Built in 1976, but renovated between 2014-2017, Qatar's national stadium is part of the Doha Sport City complex. The Hamad Aquatic Centre and Aspire Academy are also on site, but the most striking feature is the 300ft high Aspire Tower.

Also known as 'The Torch Doha' due to the way it is shaped like a flame at the top, it's Qatar's tallest building and a skyscraper hotel. It was lit-up for Liverpool's clash against Monterrey with red and white being the most prominent of the colours.

Inside the 45,000-plus capacity, dome-shaped stadium, with single tiers behind both goals and double-tiered stands along the sides, the running track used in the sparsely-attended World Athletic Championships a few months earlier was covered in faux green turf. The seats, maroon-and-white in keeping with Qatar's national colours, were far away from the pitch.

There was also the unusual sight of giant air vents, built into the base of the stands, pumping out cool air in the direction of the pitch. It wasn't particularly needed in December – a pleasant 19-24 degrees for most of the week – and created the rather odd experience of the stadium getting warmer at full-time when the air con was switched off.

Central American champions Monterrey had a small

but vociferous posse of fans behind one goal with the travelling Kop at the other end. A 'Liverpool: European Royalty' banner caught the eye. It soon became clear that Mo Salah was the biggest attraction of all.

A huge number of Egyptian fans, some of them ex-pats, were inside the Khalifa. The noise when Salah entered the pitch to warm up was reminiscent of Beatlemania.

His fan club were also enticed by the matchday DJ who took a break from dropping bangers to proclaim: "Who has come to see Mohamed Salah? Let's get this party starteddddddddd!"

You don't get that with George Sephton at Anfield, nor do you get Jordan Henderson playing at centre-half. But with Virgil van Dijk sidelined through illness and every other centre-half, bar Joe Gomez, recovering from injuries back home, the skipper had to fill in. As did James Milner at right-back.

Salah proved to be the architect for Liverpool's opening goal. Twelve minutes were on the clock when he played a pass for Naby Keita to run onto and the Guinean slotted home his third goal in three games. Two minutes later and the Mexicans were level, Rogelio Funes Mori netting from a rebound after Alisson denied Jesus Gallardo.

It was a reminder that Monterrey were no mugs and as the game developed Alisson was forced to make a number of saves, while Klopp got a booking for disputing a decision by Chilean referee Roberto Tobar, who wasn't the only erratic official the Reds would encounter in Qatar.

A second-half Mexican wave going around the stadium would normally symbolise a dull game, but if ever there was a time for one it was when the Reds were playing Mexicans!

It looked like there would be extra-time for such festivities to continue, with the game deadlocked at 1-1, until substitutes Alexander-Arnold and Roberto Firmino combined to conjure up a stoppage-time winner. A slide-rule Trent pass caught Monterrey out at their near post and Bobby nudged the ball home to send Liverpool into the FIFA Club World Cup final.

"It was always going to be a tough game," Adam Lallana, Liverpool's holding midfielder for the night, said afterwards. "They had won something to get to Qatar and teams from Central and South America play differently, but you've got to deal with different dynamics."

Copa Libertadores champions CR Flamengo had

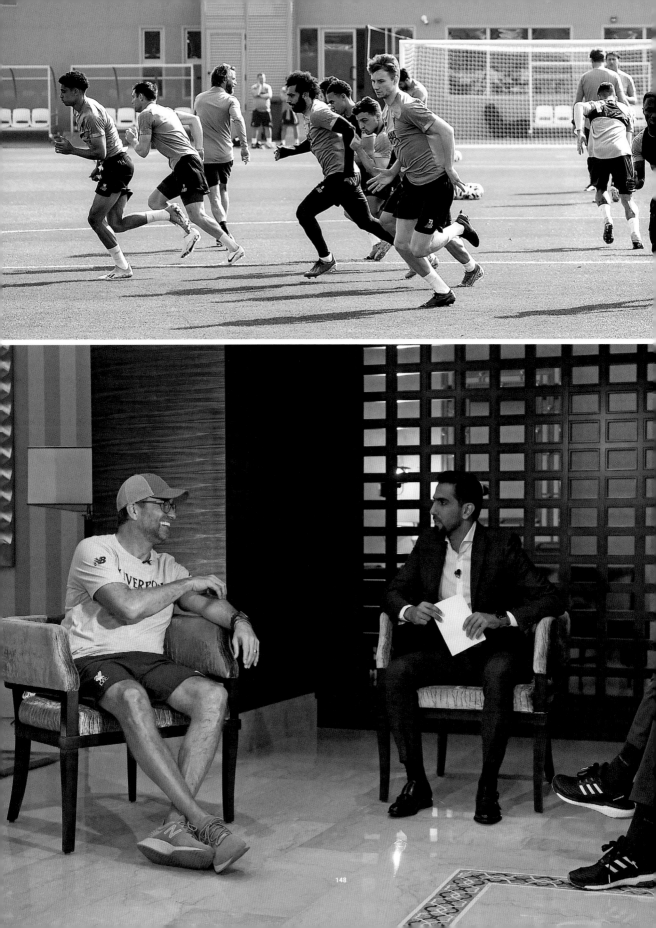

sealed their place in the final 24 hours earlier, courtesy of a 3-1 victory against Saudi Arabia's Al-Hilal, so Liverpool's victory set up a rematch of the 1981 final. The boys from Brazil won that encounter 3-0 in Tokyo against Bob Paisley's Reds, but this was to be Liverpool's time to make history.

For once, however, the travelling Kop found themselves outnumbered at a cup final. Flamengo fans were everywhere. From hotel breakfast rooms to the souqs and Corniche – they proudly wore their club's distinctive red-and-black and made themselves heard. An estimated 15,000 had travelled from Brazil – a 20-hour journey via indirect flights – because, in the eyes of many, it was the biggest game in Flamengo's history.

Beat Liverpool and they would hold the Campeonato Brasileiro Serie A (Brazilian league title), Copa Libertadores (South American Champions League) and FIFA Club World Cup at the same time – a treble they'd never previously done. It added to the perception that the tournament is considered far more important in South America than Europe.

"My friends didn't even know when the Monterrey game was or what time it was kicking off," admitted Alex Oxlade-Chamberlain. "They never miss a minute when Liverpool play – they're always checking in – so that summed it up.

"I don't want to come across as arrogant or big-headed, but I think the prize of potentially beating the European champions gives it a higher pedigree in other countries on other continents.

"A lot of those players don't get the opportunity to play the likes of Real Madrid, Barcelona, Bayern Munich or ourselves in any club competition other than the Club World Cup. Historically, the best players play in Europe at some point in their career at one of the big teams in Spain, Germany, Italy or England.

"So, when you speak to the South American guys – or the African guys – in our squad, their route as footballers was always to get to Europe to play for one of those teams. They probably hold the attraction of playing against the champions of Europe a bit higher than we do the other way around.

"That's not to be disrespectful, it's just the way the footballing world has gravitated towards the Champions League. That's what makes the Club World Cup bigger in other countries than it is over here, but at the same time

if you're lucky enough to qualify for the competition then it becomes massive to try to win it."

The Flamengo end inside the Khalifa International Stadium was packed 90 minutes before kick-off. Many had gone inside early to watch the third-place play-off, Monterrey beating Al-Hilal on penalties following a 2-2 draw.

The first player to emerge for the pre-match warm up was Alisson. The Brazilian was roundly booed by the Brazilians. So too were the rest of the Liverpool team when they emerged from the tunnel. But Salah, just like before the semi-final, was cheered loudly.

Chants of 'Li-ver-pool!' clap-clap-clap were accompanied by the beat of a drum.

A pre-match light show, with the floodlights switched off, followed. The lights had barely been switched back on when Firmino should have given Liverpool the lead in the 41st second, but he scooped Alexander-Arnold's pass over the crossbar.

Keita struck a shot over five minutes later and Alexander-Arnold sent a fizzing effort narrowly wide, but it soon became clear that Flamengo wanted to make the game a scrappy affair littered with niggly fouls, off-the-ball incidents and gamesmanship. Frustratingly, Qatar-based referee Abdulrahman Al Jassim seemed unwise to these dark arts and booked only Sadio Mane for reacting to being blatantly manhandled by Rafinha.

Two minutes after the restart, Firmino came even closer when his shot hit the inside of the post and bounced back across goal. Flamengo were riding their luck.

Alisson had to save from Gabriel Barbosa, Oxlade-Chamberlain was forced off with an ankle injury and Salah had a goal ruled out for offside before Flamengo goalkeeper Diego Alves tipped a Salah effort over. The former Valencia keeper was also mysteriously struck down by repeated bouts of cramp whenever Liverpool were getting into their stride!

Then came a dramatic finale. With a minute of stoppage-time played, Mane ran through and seemed set to score until being impeded by Rafinha on the edge of the box. The referee pointed to the spot and booked the full-back but was surrounded by Flamengo players demanding VAR be consulted.

Replays showed that Mane was marginally outside the box but was fouled. A free-kick and red card for Rafinha appeared inevitable, but after looking at the pitchside monitor the official awarded an uncontested drop-ball to Flamengo. The smile on Klopp's face was one of bemusement.

Extra-time was needed to settle it, and in the 99th minute Firmino did precisely that.

Henderson sent Mane away with a brilliant pass and he in turn gave the ball to Bobby. Liverpool's no9 calmly turned back inside centre-half Rodrigo Caio, sending goalkeeper Alves to the ground at the same time, before he fired the ball into the net. One-nil Liverpool.

Firmino whipped his shirt off in celebration – something you can only do in Qatar on a football pitch – and sprinted to the touchline before he leapt into the air. Within moments his song rang around the Khalifa. Never before had 'the best in the world is Bobby Firmino' sounded more apt.

The goal miraculously cured Diego Alves' cramp, but Flamengo created just one opportunity to equalise. Substitute Lincoln lifted a clear-cut chance over Alisson's crossbar and when the final whistle blew, Liverpool Football Club, for the very first time, were champions of the world.

"It is Bobby's quality, his moves, and he is really calm in front of goal," said Alisson when asked about Firmino's winner. "He trains like that, so when you train like that and you are concentrating, you arrive on the pitch and you do the right things. I'm really, really happy that he scored. He's a guy who deserves everything and we are really happy."

On the pitch Liverpool players celebrated. Around the world Liverpool supporters celebrated. Salah was presented with the adidas Golden Ball and Alibaba Cloud player of the tournament awards at full-time before the longest presentation ceremony in the world saw Monterrey reappear to receive bronze medals before Flamengo were handed silver. Then the Reds entered stage left.

One by one, Liverpool's players had a gold medal draped around their necks before Henderson was handed the distinctive silver and gold trophy by FIFA president Gianni Infantino.

The skipper did his trademark 'Henderson Shuffle' – no captain in world football has got quicker feet on a podium – before he turned away from his team-mates and lifted the trophy high into the Qatari sky as ticker tape blasted out behind him.

FIFA CLUB WORLD CUP

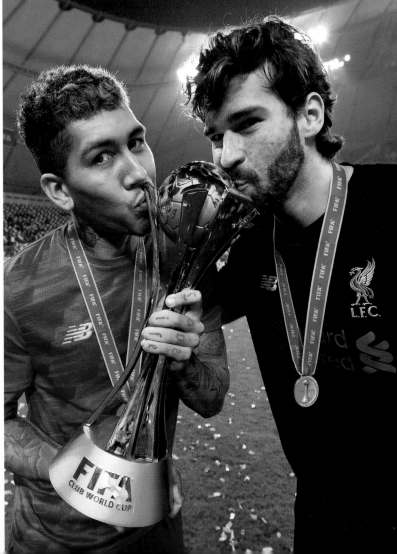

The Reds were on top of the world.

"It's a wonderful night for us, the club, for everybody who is with us," said Klopp. "I said before the game I don't know exactly how it would feel to win it. Now I can say it's outstanding, absolutely sensational."

Another trophy added to the collection, and back on Merseyside the Reds had done some shrewd Christmas shopping.

Japanese international Takumi Minamino, who had played so well against Liverpool in the Champions League for Red Bull Salzburg, had agreed terms with LFC after the two clubs negotiated a transfer fee.

After passing a medical, and being handed the no18 shirt, it was announced that he would become Liverpool's first-ever Japanese player on New Year's Day.

"It has been my dream to become a Liverpool player and I'm so excited that the moment has come true," said the 24-year-old attacking midfielder. "To play in the Premier League was one of my targets. I think this is the top-class league in the world.

"I was thinking if my career as a footballer progressed smoothly, someday I would be able to play in the Premier League. But I never thought I would be able to play in this team and I'm really happy about it. I'm looking forward to it."

The Christmas presents didn't stop there. FIFA announced that Club World Cup champions Liverpool could now wear their gold FIFA Champions badge for the next 12 months, although Premier League rules meant this would only be in the Champions League and FA Cup, excepting a specially-granted one-off in the next home game against Wolves.

"As per the usage guidelines, the winning team can wear the FIFA World Champions badge from the day it becomes champions up to and including the final of the next edition of the tournament," said a FIFA spokesman. Kopites were soon getting it added to their replica shirts at Liverpool FC's official club stores.

On Christmas Eve, a beautiful new decoration went up at Melwood. For the third time in 2019, the Champions Wall in the foyer of Liverpool's training ground was updated, with the FIFA Club World Cup becoming the 47th major honour – an English record – added to an already-prestigious list.

Champions of Europe. Super Cup holders. World Champions. Merry Christmas indeed.

IDENTITY AND MENTALITY

6

BACK WITH A BOUNCE AS THE
FESTIVE SCHEDULE KICKS IN

Christmas in the football calendar may be seriously hectic, but it's also the time to give something back. The week before the Reds flew to Qatar, they made their annual visit to Alder Hey Children's Hospital to meet patients and staff. Jürgen Klopp and his players also gave out LFC goodie bags while the Champions League trophy was on display for photos.

Back at Anfield there was an annual carol service organised by the club's Red Neighbours community team as well as a week of Christmas dinner get-togethers for local pensioners.

Back to the action on the pitch, and from the moment the 2019/20 fixture list was released it was clear that the Reds' participation in the FIFA Club World Cup would have a significant impact upon their season.

Only one league game was postponed as a result of Liverpool's duties in Doha, an away fixture at West Ham United originally set for Saturday 21 December. But only five days after they triumphed in Qatar they were back in Premier League action at Leicester City on Boxing Day. First v second.

The trip to the King Power Stadium was the first of three league games in the space of a week as the squad were expected to re-adjust back to the English winter after a trip of almost 3,500 miles. Making that transition as proficiently as possible was something the staff had been planning as best they could for several months.

In the matchday programme, assistant-manager Pep Lijnders admitted as much. "It is important [to adapt] with a 'culture of victory' because each prize we can win is important, so we try to attack each competition we play.

"But for me the most important thing is the chance to show, in a different part of the world, our identity and our philosophy and a real spirit of initiative. In a perfect world people should look forward to seeing us play.

"As regards changing between England and Qatar, we already have the people in charge who are preparing to make this process as smooth as possible. We have to ignore what's beyond our control, whatever the circumstances. This is what we always try to do, but in these periods it will be even more the case."

He added: "Of course it's different when you come back as the winning team, that's for sure! For me the most important aspect is to keep the team fresh during this period, knowing that what puts us above the rest is our mentality. We will always focus on what we can control."

When the Reds did report back to Melwood they found a welcome new addition to the reception area. The engravers had been back to make a third revision in 2019 to the Champions Wall as a first-ever FIFA Club World Cup title was added to the honours list.

Liverpool, though, had come back to one of the toughest challenges of their season, broadcast live to the nation on Amazon Prime on Thursday 26 December.

High-flying Leicester City, 9-0 winners at Southampton in late October, were the team closest to them in the table. Despite losing 3-1 away to Manchester City five days earlier they had leapfrogged the defending champions into second spot.

The big question was: how would the Reds react

against Brendan Rodgers' in-form Foxes in the midst of such a mad schedule? Could Leicester, who emerged onto the field to a light-show and pyrotechnics, capitalise and reduce Liverpool's lead at the top of the table to seven points?

Klopp's men provided all the answers in emphatic style, producing one of their best performances of the season to sweep aside their hosts with a devastating display of attacking football.

The 4-0 win stretched their lead at the top of the Premier League table to 13 points. It was also the biggest margin of victory in a match between teams starting the day in the Premier League top two since Manchester City won 6-1 at Manchester United in October 2011.

A narrow half-time advantage, courtesy of Roberto Firmino's header from a magnificent cross by Trent Alexander-Arnold, did not reflect Liverpool's superiority.

But they turned the screw after the break.

Leicester had been enjoying their best spell when centre-back Caglar Soyuncu handled inside his own area in the 71st minute. Substitute James Milner scored from the spot with his first touch seconds after coming on. It was his second successful penalty of the season against the Foxes.

Man-of-the-match Alexander-Arnold then set up another for Firmino, who scored with a cool finish. It was the 500th goal the Reds had scored under Klopp in all competitions. Finally Trent capped his own excellent performance with the fourth goal of the night, a thumping, right-footed, angled drive.

The BBC Sport homepage described the performance as "a masterclass. The leaders have now dropped only two points from their first 18 games and, having lost only one league game last season, it would take a collapse of unthinkable proportions from an outstanding team to cast this huge advantage aside.

"Liverpool have had too many near-misses since their last title win in 1990 to get ahead of themselves – but how can anyone see beyond them this time? They are in no mood to be denied."

Former Reds boss Rodgers was magnanimous in defeat: "We played our last two games against two of arguably the best teams in the history of the Premier League," he said.

"Credit to Liverpool, they played well. We just didn't have long enough periods with the ball. When you don't [do that] against a top team – world champions – it becomes difficult for you. People were trying to put us in a race with Liverpool but we know where we are."

Klopp declared: "I am happy. I appreciate it because I do not take it for granted and the boys have to do it

every three days. We were very concentrated and the goals were absolutely nice. It was an important day for us."

Guardian correspondent Barney Ronay summed up Liverpool's dominance and lauded the impact of their right-back: "Joyful and, indeed, triumphant. The King Power Stadium was a boisterous place with Liverpool's world champions in town.

"New-build stadiums can often be deathly places. Not this one, with its operatic pre-match fanfare, its sense of high-end underdog glamour and with a Leicester team unbeaten at home in the league this season. At which point, enter the red machine and, in particular, another extraordinary, incisive and deeply unusual performance from Alexander-Arnold.

"Every week the Premier League team-sheets seem to make the same category-mistake with Liverpool's defence. Liverpool's no66 plays (it says here) at right-back. In reality Alexander-Arnold is something else,

a 21-year-old footballer whose talent has redefined his role, creating in the process something new and excitingly disruptive.

"Alexander-Arnold made two goals, scored Liverpool's last one in a 4-0 win and looked irresistible at times. He is an extraordinary player in so many ways, a full-back who operates at a constant level of creative urgency."

The day after the victory, Klopp sought to boost his injury-hit central defensive resources by recalling Nathaniel Phillips from his loan at VfB Stuttgart on a short-term basis. Also incoming, a little later on New Year's Eve, was new signing Takumi Minamino to officially meet his new manager and train with his new team-mates at Melwood.

The tests kept on coming: a double-header at home to first Wolverhampton Wanderers then Sheffield United.

For the visit of Nuno Espirito Santo's impressive Wolves on Sunday 29 December, the Reds would be wearing the gold FIFA champions badge. It would also

adorn their shirts for the remaining matches in the Champions League and FA Cup.

A first-half goal from Sadio Mane proved the difference in a hard-fought encounter. VAR again had a part to play in the result. Mane's goal, initially ruled out for an assumed handball by Adam Lallana in the build-up, was subsequently awarded by VAR to the clear frustration of the visitors.

Wolves' temperatures rose even further when they then had an 'equaliser' by winger Pedro Neto chalked off on the stroke of half-time following another VAR check which ruled that wing-back Jonny was marginally offside in the build-up.

The hosts had to dig deep after the interval but another strong defensive display saw them take the three points.

"It was a tough test and rightly so," admitted Klopp post-match. "First-half we were good and controlled the game, but I can imagine Wolves were not happy with the VAR decisions. However, the momentum went with them after that moment. We had nothing to do with the decisions.

"The second half, they changed a bit. We were not fresh enough in mind to react. Football is like life. Sometimes you are 100 per cent ready and sometimes not. It was a big fight."

Virgil van Dijk was a happy man after helping the team sign off for the year on a winning note in what was his 100th appearance for the Reds: "Obviously we can be positive about the situation we're in, but we can't be satisfied.

"So far we're in the middle of the season so we want to achieve more and more. The only thing we can do now is make sure we focus on the next game and it will be a tough one again."

On becoming the club's latest centurion he added: "From my debut until now, I've been playing a lot of games and I'm very proud that I've stayed fit. Most of the games I've been on a consistent level as well, so I'm very happy about that. Obviously sometimes you could always be better but I'm not a robot."

This latest victory had seen Liverpool end 2019 with a 13-point advantage at the top of the Premier League. At the halfway stage of their league campaign they had

registered 18 wins and a draw from their 19 fixtures. As Klopp himself might have said, not bad!

Scorer Mane was thriving on his link-up with fellow forwards Salah and Firmino.

"I always say it is very easy to work together," he told the club's official magazine. "Personally I just think myself very lucky to play alongside these great players – they make everything easy, so I just enjoy playing alongside them.

"We are all from different countries and speak different first languages but I think football is one language and it is universal so everybody can speak it. It is the same with Mo, Bobby and myself."

Mane was one of only two players [Leicester's Jamie Vardy being the other] to be directly involved in 30 Premier League goals during 2019 with 24 strikes and six assists.

"It has been a fantastic year," he continued. "I think even if we hadn't won the Club World Cup it had already been a great year, but to win that trophy for the first time for Liverpool is very special. So we are happy with 2019.

"But, of course, it could still be even better and we hope we can win more trophies in the new year."

So to Thursday 2 January 2020 and Sheffield United at home. Klopp was asked about possible squad rotation to deal with the punishing schedule. "It's only one thing you think about; how do you change a line-up because of freshness? Yes, when you feel it's really busy then you have to make changes, but in other situations what we try to make sure is the pieces we put on the pitch fit together.

"So, when we played Everton at the beginning of last month and made five or six changes, we were sure this offensive line, for example, would click together. That's why we did it."

On the morning of the game against the Blades it was announced that Alisson Becker, who'd kept four consecutive clean-sheets in the Premier League, was the winner of the 2019 Samba Gold award for the best Brazilian player in Europe.

He also became the first goalkeeper to win the prize, selected by a combined poll of fans, journalists and former players, with over 35 per cent of the vote. He finished ahead of Reds team-mate Firmino, the 2018 winner (23 per cent) and Thiago Silva, who was third (10 per cent). Liverpool midfielder Fabinho was fourth.

On the pitch Alisson helped the Reds to another shut-out as they started 2020 with a polished performance to defeat Sheffield United 2-0. A goal in each half from Salah and Mane proved enough to take the Reds' advantage at the top of the table back to 13 points.

Andy Robertson set up Salah for the opener after four minutes, following a slip by Blades defender George Baldock, before Mane made things safe when he finished at the second attempt after being played in by Salah.

After the game Robertson called it "a really controlled performance. We know how we struggled at Bramall Lane [back in late September] and it was only really from a mistake that we didn't draw it. They have picked up points in every away game apart from Man City and us. They are a fantastic team, they have lit up the Premier League and are a very good squad.

"So we knew how hard it was going to be, but the early goal was crucial for us. That killed their momentum and spirit a bit, and gave us the confidence to keep the ball, pass it about a bit and create more chances.

"It could have been a lot more comfortable but 2-0 is great. A clean-sheet and two fantastic goals, three points and back to 13 clear."

"IT'S BEEN A FANTASTIC YEAR BUT IT COULD STILL BE BETTER AND WE HOPE TO WIN MORE TROPHIES"

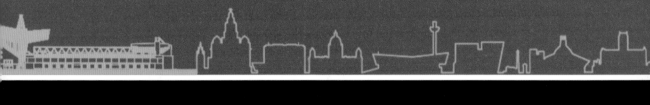

Sheffield United manager Chris Wilder was generous in his praise after seeing his side beaten in front of the Kop: "Every time we tried to press they played around us with the quality they have got. All the stuff that gets talked about in academies, with young coaches – just look at what they did in terms of the basic stuff that gives you an opportunity to play and dominate. That's what they did to us. Not only technically, but tactically, they are a fantastic side. We have been well beaten.

"People talked about us having afternoons and nights like this when we came to the Premier League. We have not had that done to us all season until now so that's a small comfort. But it still hurts, we are still professionals."

The victory also secured Liverpool's place in the history books: they became only the third team in Premier League history to go a calendar year without defeat in the competition.

The Reds had played 37 league games and picked up 101 points since losing 2-1 at Manchester City on 3 January 2019. Previously, Arsenal, whose 49 games included the entire 2003/04 season, and Chelsea, from October 2004 to November 2005, were the others to achieve the feat.

Returning from Qatar to take nine points out of nine from three tough games underlined both the Reds' quality and mentality and had much of the media purring.

The *Independent*'s Melissa Reddy wrote: "A club-record haul of 97 wasn't enough to seal the title last season and that painful near-miss has sparked a state of no surrender from this side.

"Liverpool can afford to drop points but refuse to. The champions of Europe and of the world are another game closer to claiming the status they have coveted above all for three decades: champions of England."

The Reds had a nine-day gap before their next league engagement at Tottenham Hotspur and at this point Klopp felt it was right to give his senior stars a breather. The manager had strong words about the demands being made upon players after those three full rounds of Premier League games were scheduled between 26 December and 2 January.

For the second time in three years, Liverpool had been drawn at home to neighbours Everton in the third round of the FA Cup. And in his programme notes for the fixture Klopp was unequivocal: "No-one is saying we can't play the games. The question should be: is it right to and what is the impact on health and quality?

"For me the consequences are clear. It is the players and fans who ultimately suffer and football without these two groups is nothing.

"If you follow a club and you make sacrifices, both in terms of personal finances and the even more precious commodity of time, then it is only right that you see a team give their very best. The present circumstances makes that difficult to do constantly. We still try of course.

"We pile more and more expectations onto the players. We want them to be faster, stronger, braver, smarter. We want to see them at full-throttle. And of course this should be the case – it's what the supporters deserve. But it is not possible to do this constantly without reasonable rest and recovery time.

"Players are human beings – we would all do well to remember this I think."

With that in mind the boss made nine changes as he named a very young XI for the showdown with the Toffees, who were now under the management of Carlo Ancelotti.

When the team-sheets came in, Everton were made strong favourites to end a run without a win at Anfield which dated back to 1999. But the junior Reds were not willing to lie down. Despite a few early scares, they showed their quality and went on to win 1-0 to the delight of a buoyant home crowd.

Liverpool-born teenager Curtis Jones was the match-winner with a brilliant curling effort from the edge of the area with 19 minutes remaining. The game also saw full debuts for centre-back Phillips and attacker Minamino, while defender Yasser Larouci also made his bow as an early substitute for the injured Milner.

Afterwards Klopp beamed: "I saw a sensationally good performance of a not-very experienced team with a lot of players playing for the first time on this kind of stage, in front of this crowd, against the opponent. It was outstanding. I loved it – I loved each second of this game.

"If you want to be a Liverpool player you have to respect the principles of this club. We cannot always play the best football in the world, but we can fight like nobody else. And as long as we use our principles, we will be a difficult opponent to play against."

Liverpool Echo reporter Paul Gorst couldn't resist recalling a famous Bill Shankly one-liner. "There is something about this famous old ground that brings out an inferiority complex in Everton," he wrote.

"It's now 23 games without victory against the local enemy on home soil. It might be a long time before the visitors are afforded a chance as presentable as this one to bring it all crashing down, too.

"Liverpool, the reigning European and world champions, are arguably the best footballing side on the planet in 2020. Their reserves, it seems, can perform a passable impression, too.

"Bill Shankly once quipped that the club had the best two teams on Merseyside: Liverpool and Liverpool Reserves. There might perhaps be some truth in that in 2020."

Overall, an excellent post-Christmas spell for all associated with the Reds.

Now they trained their focus on the next sequence of games, starting with their first trip to the new Tottenham Hotspur Stadium.

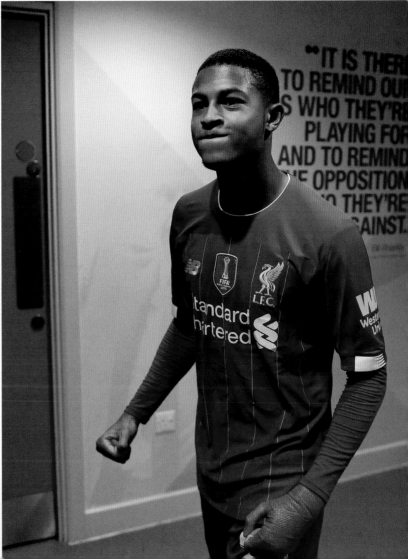

DECEMBER AWARDS

FIFA Club World Cup winners:
Liverpool FC

Barclays Premier League manager of the month:
Jürgen Klopp

Barclays Premier League player of the month:
Trent Alexander-Arnold

STANDARD CHARTERED PLAYER OF THE MONTH FOR DECEMBER:

Trent Alexander-Arnold

The right-back was a key figure as the Reds strengthened their lead at the top of the Premier League, advanced to the last 16 of the Champions League and won the Club World Cup. In eight appearances across all competitions he registered four assists and one goal.

"A good month overall. Winning trophies can only do one thing for you and that's give you a lot of confidence in terms of the ability of the team."

DECEMBER GOAL OF THE MONTH:

Mohamed Salah v RB Salzburg

Mo's geometry-defying finish in the Champions League in Salzburg ran away with it. The Egyptian made it 2-0 in the Group E encounter by rounding keeper Cican Stankovic and finishing from the tightest of angles. It beat Trent's strike at Leicester City and Divock Origi's lofted finish against Everton.

PREMIER LEAGUE TABLE 02/01/2020

	P	W	D	L	F	A	GD	Pts
Liverpool	20	19	1	0	49	14	35	58
Leicester City	21	14	3	4	46	19	27	45
Manchester City	21	14	2	5	56	24	32	44
Chelsea	21	11	3	7	36	29	7	36
Manchester United	21	8	7	6	32	25	7	31
Tottenham	21	8	6	7	36	30	6	30
Wolves	21	7	9	5	30	27	3	30
Sheffield United	21	7	8	6	23	21	2	29
Crystal Palace	21	7	7	7	19	23	-4	28
Arsenal	21	6	9	6	28	30	-2	27
Everton	21	7	4	10	24	32	-8	25
Southampton	21	7	4	10	25	38	-13	25
Newcastle	21	7	4	10	20	33	-13	25
Brighton	21	6	6	9	25	29	-4	24
Burnley	21	7	3	11	24	34	-10	24
West Ham	20	6	4	10	25	32	-7	22
Aston Villa	21	6	3	12	27	37	-10	21
Bournemouth	21	5	5	11	20	32	-12	20
Watford	21	4	7	10	17	34	-17	19
Norwich City	21	3	5	13	22	41	-19	14

7

GRINDING THROUGH THE WINTER
GEARS AND A STATUE FOR BOB

January 2020. A month which would begin with Prince Harry and his wife Meghan announcing that they planned to "step back as senior members" of Britain's royal family and end, on a less hysterical but more sombre note, with British Airways suspending all flights to and from mainland China due to the coronavirus outbreak.

On the second Saturday of the month Liverpool were travelling to Tottenham. Then it would Manchester United at home, Wolves away in midweek, an FA Cup fourth-round tie at Shrewsbury Town and West Ham away, before February began with Southampton at Anfield.

When the original fixture list for the previous season, 2018/19, had been published, the Reds were set to be the first visitors to the Tottenham Hotspur Stadium, but building delays meant the game was switched to Wembley where Liverpool won. All of which meant they'd had to wait another 16 months for their first game at the shiny new North London venue.

Half-five kick-off. Without injured talisman Harry Kane, old adversary Jose Mourinho set his side out in a deep block and invited the Reds to break them down. It would prove to be a tight affair but a first-half goal from Roberto Firmino proved decisive.

Alex Oxlade-Chamberlain had already hit a Spurs post and Virgil van Dijk's header had been saved at point-blank range by home keeper Paulo Gazzaniga. Then eight minutes before the break Firmino sidestepped home debutant defender Japhet Tanganga to let Salah's hooked pass run across his body, before beating Gazzaniga with a sweet left-footed strike.

Son Heung-Min and substitute Giovani Lo Celso missed excellent second-half chances to give Spurs some reward for a performance that improved as the game went on. But the Reds prevailed with another clean-sheet and became the first team ever in Europe's top five league games to win 20 of their first 21 league fixtures.

"We know about it and it is special but I can't feel it," said Klopp post-match. "When someone gives you a

trophy it is done, but until then you need to fight. It is only the start. We need to continue because our contenders are so strong.

"Pep [Guardiola, Manchester City boss] will not give up. I will do the same. So far, so really good."

The 1-0 victory also saw the Reds extend their unbeaten run in league action over 2019 and 2020 to 38 matches – the equivalent of an entire Premier League season.

However, left-back Andy Robertson was quick to point out that setting records would only matter if the season ended in silverware.

"For us they are irrelevant because last season we broke records in terms of clean-sheets and ended up empty-handed in the Premier League," said the Scotland captain. "Records don't mean anything unless they get you the end-goal, and hopefully this season it will.

"This league is so hard. Maybe sometimes we've made it look easy but believe me, it's not – it's so hard to perform against every team that wants to beat you. The longer the run goes on, the more everyone wants

to beat you – 'we beat Liverpool' or whatever.

"We don't take anything for granted. We are not celebrating in there [dressing-room] that we are champions. We are just celebrating a nice win just now. Long may that continue and then in May maybe we can start to celebrate."

Liverpool now had the luxury of an eight-day interval until their next fixture when traditional rivals Manchester United would make the trip to Anfield.

In the meantime there was good news for inspirational captain Jordan Henderson, who was named as the 2019 BT England Men's player of the year, seeing off competition from Raheem Sterling and Harry Kane to claim the accolade.

Henderson represented England on seven occasions during 2019 and also reached the landmark of 50 caps during a victory in Montenegro.

Further recognition came when a handful of Reds were named in the UEFA.com Fans' team of the year for 2019. Goalkeeper Alisson Becker, defenders Trent Alexander-Arnold, Robertson and Van Dijk plus Sadio

Mane all featured in the XI following an online poll. Ten Liverpool players had made the initial 50-man longlist.

Ahead of United's visit, Mohamed Salah insisted neither the occasion nor any statistical achievements mattered: "We don't think about being unbeaten until the end of the season. If we do that, it would be great, but at the end of the day we just want to win the Premier League.

"That's the most important thing. Unbeaten or not, it's not necessary – we want to win the Premier League."

Salah had not scored against United in four previous encounters and had missed October's 1-1 draw at Old Trafford with an ankle injury. This time he netted a breathtaking late goal in front of the Kop to seal a 2-0 victory.

A towering early header from Van Dijk had put the

Reds on their way but in the second half it looked like Mo had fluffed his lines when he scuffed a shot wide six yards out. In the third minute of added-time, however, he sprinted onto an astute Alisson clearance to fire past David de Gea.

The Reds goalie sprinted the length of the field to celebrate his first assist in English football, then later revealed: "I could feel my legs afterwards – it was a tough race to run!

"I did not plan the celebration, it was just something from the moment. Giving the assist to Mo is something that we try a lot in training. We tried it before when we played together at Roma but it didn't happen. Then we tried it here and it happened at Anfield in a special game, in a derby against Man United.

"It was the last minute of the game, the match was

'closed' and I just wanted to celebrate with the boys because I always celebrate by myself. It was good to celebrate but I think it was a one-off thing. We were happy it worked and if we get another opportunity we will keep trying, but I'm not running again!"

There was no doubt that Liverpool were good value for their victory having also seen a strike from Firmino ruled out by VAR for an apparent foul by Van Dijk on De Gea in the build-up.

Klopp praised his side's energy and added: "I was really happy with 85 to 90 per cent of the game. We were brilliant, we dominated, especially in the first half.

"On a normal day we would have scored three times in the first half and in the second half until 65 minutes we should have been more clear. But then United have obvious quality, played a bit more football and we had to defend.

"There were little mistakes here and there, we didn't use possession well enough and so the game stays open. Then we scored a wonderful, wonderful goal at the end – a really good feeling."

The day was also significant as, for the first time this season, a singular roar rose from the Kop regarding that three-decade wait for a league title.

"The moment came at 6.22pm on 19 January," reported the *Daily Telegraph*. "It was not when Mohamed Salah sent the ball low into the net to end any doubt that Liverpool would beat Manchester United or when Alisson sprinted from his goal to knee-slide into the celebrations and enjoy his rare assist.

"Instead it came a few seconds later when referee Craig Pawson blew the final whistle – Salah's strike proving to be the last kick of the game – with the Liverpool fans raucously chanting: 'We're gonna win the league, we're gonna win the league, And now you are going to believe us – we're gonna win the league.

"Of course they are going to win the Premier League. The wait will soon be over, the clock will soon stop, after 30 years, but this was the first time that the Liverpool supporters have allowed themselves to say that publicly. The first time they could not contain themselves any more and told the rest of the world what it already knew."

Inevitably and understandably Klopp played it down: "Everyone should celebrate the situation apart from us. Nothing has changed. We have the same situation plus three points."

And another clean-sheet, with Joe Gomez quick to praise central-defensive partner Van Dijk: "I don't think it's easy to measure what he does for us as a team. He's such a dominant character, a dominant player. He's a special player and we're lucky to have him at the club – he's my big brother!

"He's a top player and a top person to be alongside."

No let-up and next, a Thursday-night trip to Wolverhampton. The men from Molineux had given the Reds one of their toughest tests at Anfield just after Christmas and everyone in the Liverpool camp anticipating another hard night in the Black Country.

It turned out that way, too, with the visitors having to produce another resilient display at a misty Molineux to win 2-1 and, in the process, take their unbeaten sequence in the Premier League to 40 games.

An early Henderson header from a Trent corner was cancelled out after the break by a fine counter-attack which ended with striker Raul Jimenez nodding in an equaliser. It was the first league goal Liverpool had conceded in 725 minutes.

With both teams going for it, there were chances at either end before Salah wriggled free on the edge of the box and the ball broke to Henderson, who played in Roberto Firmino. The Brazilian held off a posse of markers to shoot into the corner with his left foot. It was his tenth goal of the season. All of them had come away from home. Liverpool's 'road warrior' had struck again.

The only downside was that Sadio Mane limped

off after half-an-hour with a hamstring injury. He was replaced by Takumi Minamino who made his Premier League debut.

The *Daily Telegraph* mused that talk had turned from whether Liverpool – now 16 points clear at the top of the Premier League with 15 games to go – would win the title to whether they could complete the season unbeaten.

"It seems improbable that with the resumption of their Champions League defence there will not be more injuries like Mane's [while] watching the counter-attacking combinations of Jimenez and Adama Traore, there might be others who spy a way to beat them.

"This was a night when Liverpool were not always at their best in the aspects of the game you might expect them to prevail, and yet prevail they did.

"They say that the hallmark of champions is that they win when they play badly, but no great teams have truly bad performances – just those which fall below their high standards. Liverpool were made to look vulnerable at times but they never permitted those moments to last long."

Henderson hailed the team's doggedness. "You know it's going to be difficult here as we've seen over the season – they're a good team, they make you work," the skipper told BT Sport afterwards.

"It was an intense game. We knew it'd be difficult but we knew to keep going, keep fighting. We defended really well, the big man [Van Dijk] and the back-four were brilliant again, [and] the keeper.

"We had some chances as well to put the game to bed, which I keep saying over the last couple of weeks, so that's something that we want to improve on and kill the game off earlier. But we showed mentality again to keep going and find that winning goal."

The Reds now returned their focus to the FA Cup and a televised trip on Sunday 26 January to Shrewsbury Town. Again the manager would field a young team.

Liverpool took a 2-0 lead at the Montgomery Waters Meadow through Curtis Jones then a Donald Love own-goal. But substitute striker Jamie Cummings secured a second bite of the cherry for Sam Ricketts' League One side with a penalty followed by a composed finish.

With the replay in the week that was scheduled for the Premier League's first-ever winter-break, Klopp was forthright in his reaction: he would honour the break and thus field a 'reserve' side in the Anfield return.

"Look, our situation is the following. We have known that for a couple of weeks it is like this. Actually we knew it a bit longer because it was always clear when we came through into the next round it would be like this.

"In April 2019 we got a letter from the Premier League where they asked us to respect the winter-break, not to organise international friendlies and not to organise competitive games in respect of it. I have said to the boys already, two weeks ago, that we will have a winter-break, so it means we will not be there – it will be the kids who play that game...

"I know it is not very popular, but that's the way I see it and, how I said, the Premier League asked us to respect the winter-break and that's what we do. If then the FA do not respect it then we cannot change. But we will not be there."

Three days later came a midweek trip to West Ham United in the Premier League. The fixture, postponed before Christmas with the Reds in Qatar, was Liverpool's game-in-hand and offered them the chance to extend their lead at the top of the table to 19 points.

They were always in control at the London Stadium and took a first-half lead from a Salah penalty after Divock Origi had been fouled in the box. A neat finish from Alex Oxlade-Chamberlain on the counter then clinched a 2-0 win over David Moyes' Hammers.

The triumph meant Liverpool became the first team in Premier League history to have beaten every other team in a league season, and all by the end of January.

"They're as good as there's been around," admitted Moyes. "It's very difficult to say that when you've been manager of Everton and Manchester United, but Liverpool are an excellent side." The win made it 23 out of 24 matches and took LFC's points tally to 70. But Klopp again played it down: "Yes we have 70 points, an incredible number, but so many things can happen.

"I'm not too concerned about records. We had a record

at [Borussia] Dortmund and Bayern [Munich] beat it the next season. We don't feel as though anything is done, I promise you."

Afterwards goalkeeper Alisson re-iterated the don't-stop mentality: "We always said, and we are always saying, we are focused on the next challenge and the next game. The next challenge is the most important of the season.

"We'll try to do our best to win everything. We know our qualities and we know how far we can go, but we can only go far if we do big performances on the pitch. The Premier League is top-level so you cannot stop. You just need to keep going."

The last game before the inaugural Premier League winter-break saw Southampton come to Anfield, and ahead of the fixture a bronze statue of Bob Paisley was unveiled outside the stadium.

Celebrating the life and legacy of Liverpool FC's most successful manager, and commissioned by the club's main sponsors Standard Chartered, it depicted a real moment from Bob's career when he carried the injured Emlyn Hughes from the field of play. Members of the Paisley family, along with Emlyn's daughter Emma Hughes and LFC chief executive Peter Moore, took part in the ceremony.

Back on the modern pitch Ralph Hasenhuttl's Southampton arrived as one of the league's in-form teams with a strong away-record, and they demonstrated all those qualities during a tight first-half that ended goalless.

But Alex Oxlade-Chamberlain broke the deadlock two minutes after the re-start and once Jordan Henderson doubled the advantage on the hour-mark with a calm finish after being teed up by Firmino, the Reds were in command. Salah added two further goals in the final 20 minutes.

Liverpool were now a staggering 22 points clear at the top – the biggest lead by any team at the end of a matchday in English top-flight history.

The victory also equalled Manchester City's record of 20 consecutive Premier League wins on home soil. Only Bill Shankly's Liverpool team of 1972 and early 1973 (with 21) had enjoyed a longer winning streak in the top flight on home turf.

Incredibly the Reds had earned 100 points from the last 102 available to them in the Premier League, winning 33 of their last 34 matches. Klopp was sanguine, declaring his team were "not even close to being perfect."

He continued: "We just look to use our skills in the best possible way. The boys have done that for a while pretty good and that's why we have these numbers. We didn't want a 22-point lead – we wanted 73 points at the end of today."

Firmino's personal run without a goal at Anfield had

now extended to 306 days, but he was at the heart of an exhilarating second-half display with a hat-trick of assists.

The *Daily Mail* took up the subject of the Brazilian's barren spell in front of the Kop: "Liverpool's no9 has not scored a Premier League goal at Anfield since 31 March 2019.

"In normal circumstances it would be the kind of statistic that triggers questions about how a man who wears such a famous jersey could keep his place. How can a Liverpool no9 not score at Anfield?

"Normal circumstances, however, do not apply to Roberto Firmino. It might be an anomaly that he has not registered at home since a towering header against Tottenham last spring, but nobody has a moment's worry about this Brazilian. If you needed evidence why, you simply had to watch the majesty of this performance.

"'Bobby', as the locals call him, is too good for this run of not scoring at Anfield. It is a quirk, a little foible, and in the grand scheme it will not matter if he doesn't score between now and the middle of May.

"What he has done this season is knit Liverpool's team together, the conduit for this brilliant squad to march relentlessly towards a first league title since 1990. Firmino's brilliance is there for all to behold – no goals are needed to rubber-stamp it."

There was further praise from Klopp, who said: "I do not know a player like him. He is exceptional, a very football-smart person. The good thing is he never stops being greedy to score himself in the right moment, or to pass to the guy in a better position.

"Even a player like Bobby needs an address where he can send the ball, because he cannot take the ball and turn and run alone. How he uses the skills of his mates is special."

Several of the players took advantage of the winter-break to head off to various exotic destinations (Scotland, in Andy Robertson's case!) and landed to some welcome good news: Manchester City had lost 2-0 at Tottenham, a result which saw Pep Guardiola concede the title to Liverpool.

"They are so far away, they are unstoppable," he said. "The last two seasons they said City winning the title was bad for the Premier League and it could not happen again.

"Now it's Liverpool you have to be concerned with about the Premier League."

JANUARY AWARDS

Barclays Premier League
manager of the month:
Jürgen Klopp

BT England Men's player
of the year 2019:
Jordan Henderson

UEFA.com Fans' team
of the year 2019:
Alisson Becker, Trent
Alexander-Arnold, Andy
Robertson, Virgil van Dijk
and Sadio Mane

Samba Gold award 2019:
Alisson Becker

STANDARD CHARTERED PLAYER OF THE MONTH FOR JANUARY:

Mohamed Salah

In five Premier League wins Mo contributed three goals and three assists, edging out Jordan Henderson and Alisson Becker for the prize in the online poll.

"I am happy to win this award but as I've said before many times, the important thing is to win the games – hopefully we'll keep going like that."

JANUARY GOAL OF THE MONTH:

Mohamed Salah v Manchester United

A goal which summed up everything about this team under Jürgen Klopp. Time almost up and the visitors straining every sinew to find an equaliser when sensational quick-thinking by keeper Alisson puts Mo through on goal and the roar rises as he rushes through on goal. Back of the net, Anfield erupts, we believe.

PREMIER LEAGUE TABLE 02/02/2020

	P	W	D	L	F	A	GD	Pts
Liverpool	25	24	1	0	60	15	45	73
Manchester City	25	16	3	6	65	29	36	51
Leicester City	25	15	4	6	54	26	28	49
Chelsea	25	12	5	8	43	34	9	41
Tottenham	25	10	7	8	40	32	8	37
Sheffield United	25	9	9	7	26	23	3	36
Manchester United	25	9	8	8	36	29	7	35
Wolves	25	8	11	6	35	32	3	35
Everton	25	9	6	10	31	37	-6	33
Arsenal	25	6	13	6	32	34	-2	31
Burnley	25	9	4	12	28	38	-10	31
Newcastle	25	8	7	10	24	36	-12	31
Southampton	25	9	4	12	31	46	-15	31
Crystal Palace	25	7	9	9	22	29	-7	30
Brighton	25	6	8	11	30	37	-7	26
Bournemouth	25	7	5	13	25	38	-13	26
Aston Villa	25	7	4	14	32	47	-15	25
West Ham	25	6	6	13	30	43	-13	24
Watford	25	5	8	12	23	39	-16	23
Norwich City	25	4	6	15	24	47	-23	18

"FOOTBALL IS HAPPINESS"

8

SHOCKS AND UPSETS BUT STILL
ON COURSE FOR GLORY WHEN...

Teamsheet

FA Cup
Liverpool v Shrewsbury Town
Tuesday 4th February 2020

Liverpool (Red Shirts)		Shrewsbury Town (Blue and Amber Shirts)	
62	Caoimhin Kelleher	25	Max O'Leary
46	Adam Lewis	2	Aaron Pierre
48	Curtis Jones (C)	3	Scott Golbourne
49	Liam Millar	4	David Edwards (C)
51	Ki-Jana Hoever	5	Ro-Shaun Williams
67	Harvey Elliott	7	Shaun Whalley
68	Pedro Chirivella	9	Callum Lang
72	Sepp van den Berg	17	Donald Love
76	Neco Williams	22	Sean Goss
80	Jake Cain	24	Ethan Ebanks-Landell
84	Leighton Clarkson	28	Josh Laurent

Substitutes

78	Vitezslav Jaros	1	Joe Murphy
53	Joe Hardy	6	Omar Beckles
56	Tony Gallacher	12	Ryan Sears
69	Elijah Dixon-Bonner	15	Brad Walker
77	Morgan Boyes	23	Daniel Udoh
81	Jack Bearne	35	Jason Cummings
93	James Norris	42	Sam Hart

Referee	Assistant Referees	4th Official
A. Madley	A. Holmes & N. Greenhalgh	T. Harrington

Standard Chartered · new balance · Western Union WU · AXA

www.liverpoolfc.com

February 2020 commenced, then, with the first-team squad enjoying a rare week's holiday, so it was left to Liverpool's youngsters to try to preserve the unbeaten run at Anfield.

The Reds hadn't tasted defeat on home soil since losing to Chelsea in the League Cup way back in September 2018, but Shrewsbury Town fancied their chances of victory when they arrived in L4 for an FA Cup fourth-round replay, following the earlier 2-2 draw in Shropshire.

With Jürgen Klopp taking some well-earned time away, Under-23s manager Neil Critchley took charge and in his pre-match press-conference explained what an inspiration the seniors had been to his young side.

"Sometimes it's hard to put your finger on it, but you see the culture they create. That's through the people that they are. On a regular basis it can't help but rub off on our younger players [and] I think that's been one of the biggest changes I've felt when they've had an opportunity to be in and around the senior players on a more regular basis, which a lot of them have had this season.

"When you talk about the season Liverpool are having, which is quite staggering, for our manager to still support our younger players and give them opportunity is quite remarkable really. There has been a real connection between the younger players and the first-team players and long may that continue."

Liverpool's youngest-ever line-up did themselves proud. Watched by a raucous sell-out crowd, a team with an average age of 19 years and 102 days edged out the League One side thanks to a second-half own-goal from centre-back Ro-Shaun Williams, to set up a fifth-round date at Chelsea in early March.

Afterwards Critchley could not disguise his pride: "As a coach you picture the game beforehand, you visualise it and you try to predict what's going to happen.

"Obviously with young players you're never quite sure, but I have to say from the first whistle the maturity those young boys showed to play that game was remarkable. They actually calmed me on the side and I think over 90 minutes we had the better chances and were just about the deserved winners on the night."

For midfielder Curtis Jones the evening was extra-special as he became Liverpool's youngest captain at

the age of 19 years and five days, breaking the legendary Alex Raisbeck's 120-year-old record.

"It's an amazing feeling," he said. "The boys, the coaches and the staff that have trained all week have been absolutely unbelievable and it's a proud moment for me to be the youngest to captain the Reds. I'm happy that we topped it off with a win for our great fans."

Before returning to Melwood to prepare for a Saturday trip to Norwich City then the first leg of their Champions League round-of-16 tie at Atletico Madrid the following Tuesday – hold on to your hats – the Reds added Takumi Minamino to their European squad for the remainder of the season's tournament.

The Japanese international was included among the 'A list' for the knockout stages of the competition in place of teenage defender Sepp van den Berg.

At the same time Klopp was named as the Premier League's manager of the month for January, his record-setting fifth such award of the season after the Reds opened the calendar year with five successive top-flight victories to maintain their healthy lead at the top. The boss had also received the prize for August, September, November and December.

When the senior players returned to training following the winter-break, goalkeeper Alisson Becker admitted how much he'd been enjoying the season: "It's good to be on the top. We work for this, to be on the top in a top level.

"The way we play, you need to enjoy [it] because if you don't then you cannot play all the games with our intensity. We try to do our best and be happy on the pitch. In Brazil we always say that you need to enjoy the game to be happy playing football because football is happiness."

Ahead of the long cross-country trip to East Anglia, the manager told the media that he hoped to welcome Sadio Mane and James Milner back into the fold for the match.

The duo had returned to full training after recovering from respective muscle injuries sustained during the month of January.

Indeed it was Mane who made the difference, coming off the bench to score the only goal of a tense affair, played against the high winds of 'Storm Dennis', in the 78th minute. It was his 100th goal in English football, 25 coming with Southampton and 75 for the Reds, and it gave the Reds an astonishing 25-point lead at the top.

The goal was subject to a VAR review with Norwich feeling that their defender Christoph Zimmermann was given a slight nudge by Mane ahead of his ruthless, fizzing finish, but those in charge found nothing wrong.

The Canaries had passed up a good first-half opportunity when midfielder Lukas Rupp and striker Teemu Pukki were denied by Alisson, and their manager Daniel Farke admitted afterwards that the quality of finishing was the difference between the two sides on the day.

"When I compare this chance with the situation in which Mane was able to score, our chance was much bigger but they were able to score and that's the difference in terms of individual quality. It was definitely a moment of magic [from Mane]. A world-class finish."

In the *Sunday Telegraph*, reporter Sam Wallace deemed it "a savage reminder to Norwich of the qualities of the players who are running away with the league title. It left them wondering how you stop a man capable of scoring that kind of goal within a few minutes of a comeback after three weeks away.

"It was another win for Liverpool in what has become an inevitable title season which will, on this evidence, be over very soon."

Attentions quickly switched to Spain and a return to the Wanda Metropolitano Stadium in Madrid where the Reds had been crowned champions of Europe the previous June.

From the minute the draw was made, Liverpool fans were in no doubt that the tie against Diego Simeone's rigorously-regimented side would present one of their biggest tests yet.

Gini Wijnaldum felt the teams had much in common. "They are a lot like us, fighters and also really difficult to beat," the Netherlands international told UEFA. "I think you can see that in their playing style in the competition. They are always battling to get results and they can easily switch at times when it is necessary.

"They know what they have to do to win the match. So yes, these are going to be really difficult matches."

It proved that way too with the hosts taking a narrow first-leg advantage thanks to an early goal from midfielder Saul Niguez following a corner by captain Koke. They duly defended with their lives as Liverpool dominated the ball and piled on the pressure.

Klopp, who had seen his captain Jordan Henderson limp out of the action in the latter stages, remained upbeat after the final whistle: "I have no problem with the result. If you are one-nil down at half-time in a

normal game you would say, 'Okay, we change this and this and that' and then we would give it a try.

"We will give it a try – 100 per cent – in the next game as well. I saw so many happy faces tonight from Atletico and all that stuff. I get that, because it is a big win. But it is not over yet and that's the only thing I feel.

"It's a very emotional game and we had to try to be really calm to make the right decisions and I liked a lot of parts of our game, really. Of course we have to be better in the final third and we will try it."

Defender Joe Gomez felt the taste of defeat could be used positively by Liverpool, who had suffered only their third loss of the season over 90 minutes. "It's disappointing and not something we're used to," he explained. "But if anything it just gives us that motivation to bounce back and make it right as quickly as possible.

"Sometimes it happens and you need to take the positives from it. It gives us that hunger again – not that we didn't have it but we just want to bounce back and make it right. That's what we'll try to do."

"IT'S SO SPECIAL. THE NUMBERS ARE INCREDIBLE. I SAID WE WANTED TO WRITE OUR OWN STORIES, CREATE OUR OWN HISTORY. THE BOYS TOOK THAT REALLY SERIOUSLY AND THAT IS COOL"

LIVERPOOL FC   3   21:49

WEST HAM   2   90:00

The Reds returned to Premier League action the following Monday evening, 24 February, when they hosted West Ham United. In the build-up it was confirmed that Henderson would be likely to be sidelined for around three weeks with a hamstring injury.

"Hendo, it could've been worse," said Klopp at his pre-match 'presser'. "We heard of different hamstring injuries now in the Premier League – Harry Kane, for example. It's not that bad but he will be out, I think, for three weeks, which is not cool. But how we see it, we were still lucky."

Henderson cut a frustrated figure in the Main Stand on a night when the Hammers threatened Liverpool's unbeaten league season before two goals in the final quarter saw the Reds come through as 3-2 winners.

In difficult windy conditions Wijnaldum's opener from an Alexander-Arnold cross was quickly cancelled out by centre-back Issa Diop before attacker Pablo Fornals stunned Anfield by putting David Moyes' Hammers 2-1 up early in the second period.

Liverpool trailed for around a quarter-of-an-hour before visiting keeper Lukasz Fabianski somehow allowed an effort from Salah to squirm through his legs. Nine minutes from time, the comeback was completed when assist-king Alexander-Arnold clipped a ball beyond Fabianski and Mane did the rest.

On the BBC Sport website, chief football writer Phil McNulty remarked: "The great quality of this Liverpool side, and make no mistake they got lucky with Fabianski's howlers, is that they are currently driven by an unshakeable self-belief and the error for Salah's goal tipped the balance firmly in their favour.

"It is a truly remarkable effort to have dropped only two points after 27 games and Liverpool will happily grab moments of good fortune when they can.

"Their celebrations were subdued at the final whistle, perhaps an acknowledgement of an average display, but this will not matter when in due course they are crowned champions for the first time in 30 years."

Klopp admitted that he "never thought it was possible" for his side to equal Manchester City's record of 18 consecutive Premier League victories, set between August and December 2017. "It's so special. The numbers are incredible, so difficult.

"I said we wanted to write our own stories, create our own history. Obviously the boys took that really seriously and that is all cool but just not too important at the moment. We are just in the situation and want to recover and prepare for the next game."

For local lad Alexander-Arnold there was added delight after he matched his 2018/19 tally of 12 Premier League assists with his double-contribution to the win over the Hammers.

The 21-year-old full-back also became the third-youngest player to record 25 Premier League assists in total, behind Cesc Fabregas and Wayne Rooney.

He said, modestly: "I'm happy to help the team as much as possible. That was my aim going into the season, to get over ten again. And as the season's gone on, it's been about trying to push the limits and try to break as many records as I can, try and push myself as far as I can, try and help the team as much as possible and get assists, goals and contributions.

"Obviously it's about clean-sheets first and foremost, but going forward I've tried to get as many assists as possible. I've equalled that record and now I'll look to push on and try and break it."

Around this time various football shows were debating whether the Reds could finish the Premier League season without defeat. Pundits were looking at their remaining 11 fixtures and predicting where they might just slip up.

The away games at neighbours Everton, rivals Manchester City and European place-chasing Arsenal were all potential banana-skins but it's fair to say that few had picked Watford as the place where Liverpool's invincibility might end.

Football, as the boss might say, is like that sometimes and a few sage Liverpudlians recalled the impressive display by Nigel Pearson's relegation-threatened Hornets when they'd visited Anfield in December.

What happened, though, was a real shock as a 44-game unbeaten run in Premier League action came to a juddering halt with a stinging 3-0 loss. Three second-half goals subjected the Reds to their first league reverse since January 2019 and also ended that record-equalling run of 18 consecutive league wins.

Two goals from Mane's Senegal team-mate Ismaila Sarr and another by Watford captain Troy Deeney condemned Klopp's men to a defeat which still left them 22 points clear at the top of the Premier League table!

The BBC Sport website mused: "Many had arrived at Vicarage Road expecting to see Liverpool make history by winning in the league for the 19th game in a row.

"Indeed, such was the level of expectation that press accreditation for the game had been oversubscribed, with hundreds of media outlets keen to cover a moment

in English football history. But Watford were clearly not reading from the same script."

Post-match, Klopp said: "I don't think you can break records because you want to break records. You break records because you are 100 per cent focused on each step you have to do, whatever record it is – a marathon or whatever – and for that you have to perform.

"The boys performed and that's why we won the games, but tonight we were not good enough and that's not now a plus for me that I think in history, when they look back in 500 years and say 'Liverpool nearly did it'.

"That's not my main concern, you cannot change that and it was always clear, sometime we would lose a game. We didn't wait for it, but it was clear it would happen – and tonight it happened.

"Now I see it rather positively. I am not bothered, but I am not sure other people think about it, so now we can play 'free football' again. We don't have to defend or try to get a record, we can just try to win football games again and that is what we will do."

Centre-back Virgil van Dijk was gracious in defeat, adding: "Credit to Watford, they played well, a lot of fight, very disciplined and scored three goals – that's the

reality, we couldn't find a way through. It was difficult and we have to do better.

"The record and the talk of the records is all media – we just try to win every game. We will focus on the next game, the cup game [at Chelsea], and we try to win there. We have to stay humble and work harder next game."

Despite the disappointment of the result in Hertfordshire, the run remained one of the best of all-time. Only 12 teams had gone a year or more unbeaten in Europe's top five leagues in the last century.

The Reds fell 14 games short of AC Milan's 58-game unbeaten Serie A run from May 1991 to March 1993, lasting for 672 days. However, Liverpool's was the fifth-longest in Europe's top five leagues, behind only Milan, Bayern Munich, Arsenal and Juventus.

After his match-winning display, Sarr paid tribute to his compatriot: "Sadio is not only a Senegal team-mate – he is my inspiration and my idol. For me, he is the best player in the world, certainly the best African player in Europe.

"When I first came to Watford, he sent me messages welcoming me to the Premier League and when he gives me any pieces of advice I listen carefully."

On Monday 2 March, 24 hours before the FA Cup fifth-round tie at Chelsea, it was revealed that Neil Critchley, the man who took charge of the replay win over Shrewsbury Town, was the new head coach of League One Blackpool.

Klopp again rang the changes but this time Liverpool lost an entertaining game 2-0 at Stamford Bridge. A goal from winger Willian gave the Blues a half-time advantage before fellow midfielder Ross Barkley doubled the lead with a fine solo effort after the break.

Adam Lallana reflected: "There were big moments in the first half where we failed to score. It felt like an end-to-end game, a typical cup tie, probably good for the neutral. [But] we're disappointed not to score. The second half started well, there were a couple of breaks in play and it felt like we lost our momentum a little bit.

"A couple of mistakes and if you let a good team like Chelsea counter on you like that, they're going to have chances. We're bitterly disappointed with the result but credit to Chelsea."

Around this time, talk of a possible disruption to the season surfaced with the spread of COVID-19 cases around the world.

Liverpool FC issued a statement revealing that the club had introduced several new measures across their operations to help prevent the spread of the virus and protect the health of employees.

All the Reds could do was concentrate upon returning to winning ways when they hosted Bournemouth in their 29th Premier League game of the campaign. But they had to do so without goalkeeper Alisson who would be ruled out for the foreseeable future with a hip injury.

Adrian therefore retained his place between the sticks for the visit of the Cherries but was soon picking the ball out of his net when Callum Wilson put the visitors ahead, despite what appeared to be a foul on Gomez in the build-up.

VAR allowed the goal to stand but the Reds responded in trademark fashion and were 2-1 up by the break. Salah levelled with his 70th league goal for Liverpool on his 100th Premier League appearance for the club after Mane pick-pocketed defender Jack Simpson.

The Senegalese ace then gave the hosts the advantage by keeping his cool to slot past goalkeeper Aaron Ramsdale after being found by a fine pass from Van Dijk.

Mane also hit the woodwork after the break with a spectacular strike, but the Reds were left grateful that Bournemouth defender Nathan Ake passed up a presentable chance to equalise in the closing stages.

They also needed a galloping goal-line clearance from James Milner to deny winger Ryan Fraser whose lob over Adrian looked destined for the net.

The following day's *Sunday Telegraph* reported: "A nervous hush is not what you might expect to accompany the final furlong for a team who led the Premier League by 22 points going into yesterday's games, but then there have been so few wobbles in this Liverpool season that even one defeat can do strange things to the prevailing mood.

"A losing streak of one league game was ended by Klopp's players, albeit not as confidently as the manner in which they have dispatched so many opponents at a stadium where they have now won 22 straight league games – an English top-flight record. In fact, in the last minute of regulation time, Nathan Ake might have equalised, a goal that would not have changed the title race much, other than to add to an unexpected sense of Anfield anxiety.

"Ake did not do so, and Liverpool held on for a win that puts them within three victories of that title."

Salah's goal saw him become the club's all-time overseas leading scorer in league football and the first Reds player to score 20 in three successive seasons since Michael Owen. The Egyptian also set a new club record for most goals in his first century of LFC appearances.

"He is an outstanding striker, a world-class striker," said Klopp. "It's really nice. I'm really happy for him that he reached that mark and I think Sadio has the chance to do similar stuff. That would be really cool.

"We need the boys because with all the good stuff you can do on the pitch, in the end you need somebody to finish it off and very often, thank God, it was Mo."

Manchester United's 2-0 victory over Manchester City at Old Trafford the following day meant Liverpool were now just two wins away from clinching that coveted first Premier League crown. Liverpool had their own derby coming up, scheduled for Monday 16 March at Goodison Park where they'd hope to record a hat-trick of wins against the Blues in 2019/20. But first, the second leg against Atletico Madrid in the Champions League last 16.

Andy Robertson took on the pre-match media duties and insisted that he and his team-mates would need to conjure up their "full package" if they were to progress to the quarter-finals.

"I think Atletico will come out, try to pose a threat, attack us and try to get a goal because they know they can fancy themselves to defend it. They are an unbelievable team at defending deep, at defending in the 'low block' and things like that.

"We know how tough it is going to be, we know how good they are and we really need to bring our full package against them."

On a terrifically hard-fought night the Reds drew level

on aggregate a couple of minutes before the break when Wijnaldum headed them in front. The hosts continued to dominate as they attacked the Kop after the interval but were thwarted by a series of fine saves from visiting keeper Jan Oblak.

His efforts took the game to extra-time but Liverpool seemed to have found their way past Diego Simeone's stubborn side when Firmino struck four minutes into the additional half-hour. It was his first goal at Anfield for almost a year.

The stadium was bouncing but Atletico grabbed a precious away-goal almost straight from the kick-off when Adrian miscued a clearance and substitute Marcos Llorente punished him with a ruthless finish.

Llorente struck again soon afterwards meaning the Reds needed to score twice to progress. As they pushed for those goals, Atletico countered again and sent the defending champions out of the tournament when on-loan Chelsea striker Alvaro Morata kept his composure to give the Spaniards a 3-2 win on the night.

The result also ended the manager's long unbeaten home run as Atletico became the first visiting team to win a European tie at Anfield since the German took charge in 2015.

The *Daily Telegraph*'s chief football correspondent Jason Burt wrote: "There were 26 efforts on target from Klopp's side in the 90 minutes of normal time and Oblak repelled all but one.

"It means Liverpool have gone out of the Champions League and the FA Cup within eight days and have lost four of their last six games.

"For Liverpool, this is still a historic, wonderful season and fingers crossed it will be completed despite the coronavirus crisis, as they have run away with the Premier League, but it was still a shock to see them go out of the competition and in this manner."

Klopp insisted to the press that Liverpool would "come again" in the Champions League. "We tried everything. For two-and-a-half years we had an exceptional ride in the Champions League, we had party after party after party, pretty much. And tonight was a party, everything was set, it was great – crowd exceptional, the stadium, everything showed up in the best way.

"The boys delivered a super game, fought hard, played well and scored wonderful goals. But we lost. That's it. No impact on anything."

Captain Henderson, who had returned to the starting

line-up after his injury, also acknowledged the "bitter disappointment – with the position we were in and to concede the goals we did isn't like us.

"But listen, the lads gave everything. As we always do, we left everything on the field, but unfortunately we just couldn't get the result we wanted. It'll not feel nice [for a couple of days] but we've got to use it and react in the right way and finish off the season well."

Two days later, elite football in Britain was suspended until at least 3 April as a result of the spread of COVID-19, and the club issued the following statement:

"Liverpool Football Club continues to implement the government's advice on the coronavirus outbreak and welcomes today's Premier League statement to postpone all games, including Premier League, FA Cup, academy and Women's Super League fixtures in the best interests of players, staff and supporters.

"The club has implemented its own precautions across its sites to minimise the spread of the coronavirus by minimising contact where practicable and reinforcing the official medical advice for everyone to take responsibility for excellent personal hygiene."

As the country attempted to adjust to what was quickly called 'the new normal', Klopp was praised for making a powerful statement to supporters.

He said: "I don't think this is a moment where the thoughts of a football manager should be important, but I understand for our supporters they will want to hear from the team and I will front that.

"First and foremost, all of us have to do whatever we can to protect one another. In society, I mean. This should be the case all the time in life, but in this moment I think it matters more than ever.

"I've said before that football always seems the 'most important of the least important things'. Today, football and football matches really aren't important at all. Of course, we don't want to play in front of an empty stadium and we don't want games or competitions suspended, but if doing so helps one individual stay healthy – just one – we do it no questions asked.

"If it's a choice between football and the good of the wider society, it's no contest. Really, it isn't."

On 19 March 2020, the FA, Premier League and EFL released a joint-statement confirming that the Premier League season would be extended indefinitely and that the professional game in England would be further postponed until no earlier than 30 April.

Five days later, Prime Minister Boris Johnson announced that Britain would go into lockdown with people being urged to stay at home.

Incredible football season, unbelievable times.

FEBRUARY GOAL OF THE MONTH:

Mohamed Salah v Southampton

Mo's deft finish against the Saints was the third of Liverpool's four goals in that Premier League match. He collected Jordan Henderson's pass and coolly lifted a finish over goalkeeper Alex McCarthy at the Kop end. Sadio Mane's winner at Norwich was second while Alex Oxlade-Chamberlain's low drive against Southampton came third.

STANDARD CHARTERED PLAYER OF THE MONTH FOR FEBRUARY:

Trent Alexander-Arnold

Trent saw off competition from Salah and Jordan Henderson to clinch the award for a second time in 2019/20, having also won it in December. The right-back started five of the Reds' six fixtures during the month as they strengthened their grip at the top of the table.

"I'm just grateful to be a part of the club. As a fan or a player, I feel the same things that I've always felt and that's joy after the wins and disappointment after losses. It's not just the players who are out there winning games, it's the fans too. We're all in this together. Everyone has these amazing feelings for the club so for us to be able to give something back to the fans is special."

PREMIER LEAGUE TABLE 09/03/2020

	P	W	D	L	F	A	GD	Pts
Liverpool	29	27	1	1	66	21	45	82
Manchester City	28	18	3	7	68	31	37	57
Leicester City	29	16	5	8	58	28	30	53
Chelsea	29	14	6	9	51	39	12	48
Manchester United	29	12	9	8	44	30	14	45
Wolves	29	10	13	6	41	34	7	43
Sheffield United	28	11	10	7	30	25	5	43
Tottenham	29	11	8	10	47	40	7	41
Arsenal	28	9	13	6	40	36	4	40
Burnley	29	11	6	12	34	40	-6	39
Crystal Palace	29	10	9	10	26	32	-6	39
Everton	29	10	7	12	37	46	-9	37
Newcastle	29	9	8	12	25	41	-16	35
Southampton	29	10	4	15	35	52	-17	34
Brighton	29	6	11	12	32	50	-8	29
West Ham	29	7	6	16	35	50	-15	27
Watford	29	6	9	14	27	44	-17	27
Bournemouth	29	7	6	16	29	47	-18	27
Aston Villa	28	7	4	17	34	56	-22	25
Norwich City	29	5	6	18	25	52	-27	21

9

PUTTING OTHERS FIRST BEFORE
BRINGING IT BACK HOME

250

Anfield, empty. The city-centre, deserted, dazed and confused, aside from key workers on the move and those walkers and runners taking advantage of the unseasonally fine weather. This was Liverpool in lockdown, much like the rest of the country, much like the whole world.

It lasted from late March through the whole of April and May and into June. So many lives lost and so much heartbreak, but compassion too as Liverpool FC brought together its official charity, community programme and wider club staff in a coordinated response to the COVID-19 pandemic.

Around 25,000 medically-approved face-coverings were donated by LFC Foundation to the city's health-service planners. Essential items went to new mums at Liverpool Women's Hospital, 'goodie bags' to NHS and frontline workers, and hundreds of fresh meals to firefighters, ambulance staff and school hubs. Similarly the Spirit of Shankly fan-group delivered food and essentials to the most vulnerable in the city region.

There were 'virtual cuppas' too for people at further risk of social isolation, with Jürgen Klopp, Andy Robertson and Virgil van Dijk among those ringing for a surprise chat through an initiative called LFC Connect.

Whenever possible the players engaged with fans on

social-media from their homes, often just to have fun, always to keep spirits up. Together we were indeed stronger.

No less than 105 days separated Liverpool's last Premier League game against Bournemouth at Anfield on Saturday 7 March and the first fixture of 'Project Restart' at Goodison Park re-scheduled for Sunday 21 June. It was the longest in-season hiatus since the 'Big Freeze' winter of 1962/63 when the team went 52 days without playing.

The Reds had returned to non-contact training at Melwood on Wednesday 20 May with players working in small groups. "It felt like the first day at school," admitted Klopp.

Full contact training resumed on 31 May, and in a session at Anfield the players 'took the knee' in support of the 'Black Lives Matter' movement following George Floyd's death in America.

By then the FA had announced that they would not declare the season null-and-void while the Government said it was "opening the door" for the return of professional football in England in June and "widening access for fans to view live coverage."

Even so, Jordan Henderson admitted on BBC Radio 5 Live that playing at Anfield and lifting the Premier League trophy without any supporters present would be "pretty strange."

He quickly added a note of caution: "It is still not over. We have work to do and we need to perform at a high level right the way until the season finishes."

Klopp later admitted he'd been "worried when people started talking about 'null-and-void'. I felt it physically. I was like, wow, that would have been hard. When it was off the table I felt quite relieved, but I didn't think when we went to lockdown: oh my God, that is our season, we are so close. It was not important in that moment."

There had also been talk of the 236th Merseyside derby being moved to a neutral venue for safety concerns, but after meeting supporters groups the

City Council awarded safety certificates for Liverpool and Everton to play their remaining home games at Anfield and Goodison Park respectively.

While the famous copper birds on their own perch atop the Royal Liver Building were given a checkup by intrepid maintenance crew, behind-closed-doors football returned five nights before the derby date with two games played, the second of which saw Manchester City defeat Arsenal 3-0 at home. That meant it was impossible for Liverpool to clinch the title 'across the park', to the relief of Evertonians!

Football looked very different with stadiums limited to 300 people and divided into three zones: red, including the pitch and technical areas; amber for the stands; and green for stand concourses, with restrictions on who was allowed to go where and temperature checks on arrival.

Teams were now able to make five substitutions rather than the usual three and could name nine on the bench instead of seven. Deep cleaning of corner-flags, goalposts, match-balls. No handshakes before kick-off. Water-breaks at the mid-point of each half. Post-match, pitch-side broadcast interviews using boom microphones, and virtual press-conferences.

Ahead of the derby, Klopp said via the video-conferencing software Zoom that his squad were fit, healthy and ready to go again. "We don't expect to get it [the title] as a present...so we were really happy when it was decided we could play again. That is great. That is how it should be in sports.

"You have to train even more after a longer break and that's what we were working on. It looked really good, a lot of things were still there, but timing and stuff like this always needs to be adjusted and that's what we did.

"I expect us to be in a good shape but we will see how good it is."

Trent Alexander-Arnold added: "There's a huge feeling of excitement and all the players will tell you that they can't wait to get back out there and get playing matches again."

The Liverpool squad arrived on three different buses and changed in a Portakabin on the car-park before walking out in single file to the backdrop of empty stands and a rainbow overhead.

Prior to kick-off both sets of players 'took the knee' for BLM and the show of solidarity would be repeated in all of the remaining fixtures of 2019/20.

The game itself proved to be an anti-climax with the teams struggling to find their rhythm in the empty arena, a common factor in all of the first week's fixtures, and for the third successive season it ended goalless at Goodison.

Klopp called the point "one we deserved, even when I have to admit that Everton had the biggest chance to win the game. That was a little bit our problem, that we didn't create enough chances with all the possession we had.

"I liked the intensity level of the game. I liked the high-press, counter-press, all these kind of things. I didn't like too much – but you cannot force that – the rhythm." Everton manager Carlo Ancelotti agreed that "nobody deserved to lose."

The *Times* chief football writer Henry Winter captured the oddness of the occasion: "The procession towards the title has been delayed by lockdown, but Liverpool fans know it will come. Along with Everton fans, they heeded pleas not to congregate outside Goodison Park as Project Restart continues behind closed doors.

He continued: "Only a handful of fans gathered outside, including a lone saxophonist who rotated *Love Will Tear Us Apart* with Everton's theme tune from *Z-Cars*. The strains floated into Goodison, mixing with the shouts of 'Ref', 'Hold', 'Time' and 'Brilliant, Naby!'

"The noise was missing, making the strangest of atmospheres. The Beatles in an empty Cavern. Liverpool fans particularly love Goodison as it has been a happy hunting-ground. Not yesterday. [But] Liverpool's title will come, just further delayed. What's a few more days when you've waited 30 years?"

Despite dropping points for only the third time in 30 Premier League matches, Liverpool now needed just five more to claim the title.

They had not used Mo Salah against Everton or been able to name Andy Robertson in their matchday squad

"THE PROCESSION TOWARDS THE TITLE HAS BEEN DELAYED BY LOCKDOWN, BUT LIVERPOOL FANS KNOW IT WILL COME, JUST FURTHER DELAYED. WHAT'S A FEW MORE DAYS WHEN YOU HAVE WAITED FOR THIRTY YEARS?"

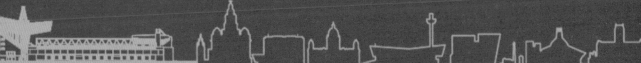

but Klopp confirmed that both were expected to be available for the subsequent midweek match with Crystal Palace at Anfield.

The following day Manchester City maintained their mathematical hopes by thrashing Burnley 5-0 at the Etihad Stadium. Klopp said: "I watched [them] and thought: how is it possible that someone is 20 points clear of this team? We must have done something right."

Meanwhile in the LFC matchday programme Virgil van Dijk admitted that playing at an empty Anfield would take some getting used to: "The supporters not being there will be so strange, particularly as they are so important to us. But like so much in this time, we have to make the best of it.

"The supporters haven't disappeared – they will just be somewhere else. We know we will have millions of people watching us from their homes so we still have the responsibility to perform for them and ourselves.

"The whole world has had to make sacrifices in the last three months or more and unfortunately the way things are at the moment means we play at the stadium and the supporters watch from their homes. But we have a

strong-enough connection to our fans to know they'll be with us for every kick, header, pass, shot and save.

"We can still make this cool if we all really give our best. The supporters know we feel them and I really hope we can help bring some joy with what we do on the pitch."

The Kop still looked fabulous, thanks to the dedication of fan-group Spion Kop 1906 and their pals. So much so, the club's own channel LFCTV released a video of them carefully adorning the stand with flags and banners, with this message from Jürgen Klopp: "When I sit in my spot in the stadium before the game starts, I always look to the Kop and it's always incredible because we have all these common experiences and memories.

"Thank you very much to everybody who puts so much soul into it – it's incredible."

On the back of four consecutive wins and clean-sheets, Roy Hodgson's Palace arrived in L4 in a fleet of people-carriers upon landing at John Lennon Airport. They'd head back home the same way.

From the first whistle there was a zip to the Reds' play that had been lacking at Goodison. With Robertson and Salah restored to the team to rekindle their link-ups with Sadio Mane and Alexander-Arnold on their respective flanks, this would be a vintage Liverpool performance.

The hosts were relentless, swarming around their opponents, forcing them into mistakes. It finished 4-0 but in truth could have been more. Palace didn't register a single touch in the Liverpool penalty area throughout the 90-plus minutes.

Klopp beamed with delight on the sidelines. "I said before we started again that I wanted to see the best behind-closed-doors games and performances," he said.

"That was certainly the best behind-closed-doors counter-pressing performance I have seen. In the 87th minute when we were four-nil up we had four players chasing after one ball. I loved that."

Alexander-Arnold opened the scoring midway through the first half with a wicked free-kick which is fast becoming his speciality, just outside the box, over the wall and beyond the helpless grasp of Eagles keeper Wayne Hennessey.

At 21 years and 261 days, Trent became the youngest player to score a direct free-kick in a Premier League game at Anfield since Robbie Fowler, aged 20 years and 252 days, against Manchester United in 1995.

The Reds doubled their advantage on the stroke of half-time with Salah making a run from the right flank in

behind the Palace defence. Fabinho picked him out with a perfectly-flighted pass which Mo chested down before clipping home. Liverpool's 100th goal of the season in all competitions.

After the break Fabinho put his own name on the scoresheet with a 25-yarder which drew comparisons with his goal against Manchester City back in November. The only thing missing was 53,000 spectators to roar in appreciation.

The *Daily Telegraph*'s Jason Burt: "This was Liverpool quickly back to their best and Fabinho returning to his stunning dominance, capped with a quite brilliant goal that had that delicious trajectory of the ball still rising as it hit the net.

"There was also the bonus of that wonderful 'ping' sound that can only be heard inside an empty stadium. Unstoppable. Utterly emphatic. Just like Liverpool this season.

"It was Jürgen Klopp's assistant, Pep Lijnders, who named Fabinho 'The Lighthouse' within the 'organised chaos' that the Liverpool manager demands... In one performance Fabinho reasserted himself as the best defensive midfielder in the league during this campaign."

Liverpool's fourth goal was also a thing of beauty, albeit in a different way – the kind of devastating counter-attack that had Klopp's fingerprints all over it. The front-three all played their part with Firmino finding Salah whose first-time pass allowed Mane to make haste towards goal before opening up body and dispatching.

There was still time for Neco Williams to make his Premier League debut and though he was only on the field for a quarter-of-an-hour, the teenage Welshman caught the eye. Flying forward from his right-back station, he even managed to fire two shots at goal: the first blocked by ex-Reds defender Mamadou Sakho and the second well-saved by his compatriot Hennessey.

Klopp told Sky Sports: "Imagine how this stadium would have been, full today, and all the people could have experienced it live. I don't think the game could have been better because my boys played like everybody was here. The atmosphere on the pitch was incredible.

"The boys are in good shape and in a good mood and it was important we showed our supporters we are still here and we do not want to wait."

Back in *The Telegraph*, writer Chris Bascombe expressed the general feeling that Liverpool's coronation was effectively done: "Jürgen Klopp can almost see his reflection glistening in the Premier League trophy now. A performance of champions against Crystal Palace took Liverpool closer to the end of their 30-year crusade."

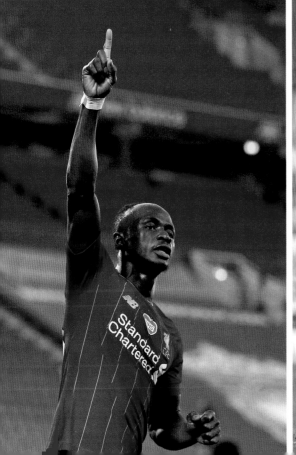

The victory was Liverpool's 23rd consecutive home league win at Anfield and left them 23 points clear of City, and it meant that the Reds would be confirmed as Premier League winners if City failed to beat Chelsea down in West London 24 hours later.

However, Alexander-Arnold insisted that Liverpool's focus remained only on themselves: "We were quite disappointed to only get the draw in our first game back at Everton. But our first game back at Anfield, after what's gone on, couldn't have gone any better to be honest. We're made-up with the win.

"We're two points away so I'd say we're close, but we've got to focus on ourselves and not take things for granted. For us, we're not really hoping that Man City drop points. We know it's in our hands so whatever happens between Chelsea and City, we still have to go to City next Thursday and try and get a result.

"Obviously we've still got a lot of games left in the season so we want to keep pushing ourselves and maybe set a few records along the way."

Former Liverpool captain and manager Graeme Souness told Sky Sports that if he were a Reds player he'd want to win the title by beating City at the Etihad the following week. In the event, though, goals from two men formerly linked with possible moves to the club, Christian Pulisic and Willian, gave Chelsea a 2-1 win at Stamford Bridge.

And so, at just after 10pm on Thursday 25 June 2020, the wait of 30 years and almost two months came to an end. Liverpool were champions of England again.

The Liver Bird was back on its perch.

The Reds squad had gathered at the Formby Hall Hotel a few miles north of the city, to enjoy a barbecue and watch the game together, and there were jubilant scenes captured on social-media when referee Stuart Attwell blew his whistle to signal the end of the game and that three-decade-long wait. Party most definitely on.

"I called my family, I think, ten seconds before the final whistle," Klopp revealed at the virtual press-conference the next day. "We had a Facetime call. I told them I loved them. They told me they loved me. We could not be together – that's not nice but that's how it is.

"I then put the phone on the table and said, 'Leave it on because in the next five seconds, something nice can happen!' They watched the game, so they knew it."

As Klopp and his players danced in delight, Liverpool's locked-down fans around the world celebrated in their own ways: madcap, tearful, perhaps even a few pensive, just-let-it-sink-in moments.

Among them was Sir Kenny Dalglish, the man who had led the Reds to their previous title success in 1989/90. Raising a glass of champagne he said: "Bob Paisley chose not to drink after some of the team's successes and said he just wanted to drink in the moment. I am not following his advice!"

Sir Kenny also paid tribute to Klopp as an emotional Reds boss joined him and Souness via video-link on Sky Sports. "The levels of consistency your team achieve is truly incredible," Souness told him. "They don't just do it eight or nine times out of ten, they do it ten times out of ten which is remarkable."

Typically Klopp put the focus on his players and staff, saying the following day: "The last 13 months have been pretty special for us, that's absolutely true, and I would like to include the year before as well because that was just an incredible football-time in my life, to be honest.

"Winning the amount of games, getting this amount of points is absolutely exceptional and I didn't experience it before. I've had good parts during my career but not that good, so I couldn't be more thankful. The consistency the boys showed is so exceptional I cannot describe it – and we will not stop.

"What I can promise is that we will try everything to improve and that's possible because there are football parts we can improve.

"[With] this group, it's the mix. Yes, we have a lot of really, really good players, world-class players, but other clubs have world-class players as well. The consistency comes from the mix with determination, with buying into the idea, with attitude, character, with personality. That makes the difference and that is what makes this group so special.

"They are all very confident meanwhile of course because we won some stuff, but they are still humble. As long as we stay humble we have a good chance to be successful in the future as well."

Captain Jordan Henderson, who had steadfastly refused to talk about the team's title chances throughout the season, could finally lower his guard. "I could never in words describe the feeling of winning the Premier League, just like I couldn't describe winning the Champions League," he said.

"It's a unique feeling and one that, again, I'm very proud of. I've been so honoured to be part of this football club right from the first moment that I came, and to go on the journey with this manager, this group of players, these fans – it's been so special.

"It's hard to describe, to be honest. But after the final whistle [of the Chelsea-City game] it was just an amazing feeling to spend it with all the lads and the staff. To finally get over the line is a relief but also amazing."

Writing in the following day's *Guardian*, the wonderfully whimsical Barney Ronay summed it up like this: "No asterisks. No caveats. And let's face it, no contest. For the last few months a theory has been doing the rounds that the ersatz nature of the Premier League end-game, five weeks of press-ganged summer ghost-ball, would drain the colour from Liverpool's first league title in 30 years.

"Fat chance. Death, plague and economic collapse may have stalked the land, puncturing sport's ability to pretend the rest of the world is simply a subplot. But sport has many functions beyond simply flag-waving and Liverpool's success will be deeply felt at a club where, as with every other club, football has always been a bit more than just football.

"This was annihilation. Liverpool didn't just outrun the rest of the field. From late summer into spring they seemed to be operating to a different set of physical laws, marching the Premier League around in a headlock, rustling its hair, flicking its ears.

"Here's a team that won 26 of 27 league games from August to 28 February; that haven't lost at home in the league in three years; a group of world champions whose best player is an unfussy centre back, whose centre-forward can't score at home, whose most creative force is a junior right-back, who have spent £92 million net on transfer fees in the last five years. This is not the standard version of annihilating success."

Klopp allowed his players a couple of days off. On the following Sunday, 28 June, they reported back to Melwood for training, and for the first time as champions.

BACK ON OUR PERCH

JUNE AWARDS

BBC Match of the Day goal of the month for March/June: **Fabinho v Crystal Palace**

PREMIER LEAGUE TABLE 30/06/2020

	P	W	D	L	F	A	GD	Pts
Liverpool	**31**	**28**	**2**	**1**	**70**	**21**	**49**	**86**
Manchester City	31	20	3	8	77	33	44	63
Leicester City	31	16	7	8	59	29	30	55
Chelsea	31	16	6	9	55	41	14	54
Manchester United	32	14	10	8	51	31	20	52
Wolves	32	13	13	6	45	34	11	52
Tottenham	31	12	9	10	50	41	9	45
Burnley	32	13	6	13	36	45	-9	45
Sheffield United	31	11	11	9	30	31	-1	44
Arsenal	31	10	13	8	43	41	2	43
Crystal Palace	32	11	9	12	28	37	-9	32
Everton	31	11	8	12	38	46	-8	41
Southampton	32	12	4	16	41	55	-14	40
Newcastle	31	10	9	12	29	42	-13	39
Brighton	32	7	12	13	34	44	-10	33
Watford	32	6	10	16	29	49	-20	28
West Ham	31	7	6	18	35	54	-19	27
Bournemouth	31	7	6	18	29	50	-21	27
Aston Villa	32	7	6	19	36	60	-24	27
Norwich City	31	5	6	20	25	56	-31	21

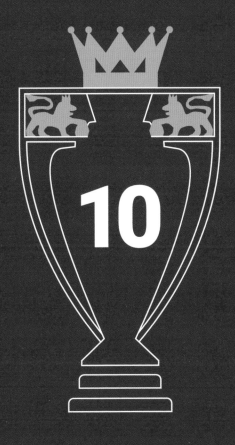

10

FINISHING THE SEASON WITH
FIREWORKS AND FABULOUS FOOTBALL

Seven days after being crowned champions, Liverpool had a rare bad day in the office. Manchester City are always dangerous opponents, but with the Reds having so convincingly overhauled the single-point gap between the two sides twelve months previous, Pep Guardiola's men were out to prove a point at the Etihad.

City welcomed the new champions onto the pitch with a guard of honour, all but one of their players applauding. In the event they won 4-0.

Had Mo Salah's shot gone in rather than struck the upright with the game goalless it might have been very different, but nonetheless Jürgen Klopp faced some difficult questions at full-time.

"If you want to lead this story in the direction [that] we were not focused, then do it," he bristled to Sky Sports.

"I liked my team's attitude. Isn't it nice another team

can be champions when Man City can play so well?"

Relegation-threatened Aston Villa were up next and arrived on Merseyside with ex-Reds keeper Pepe Reina making his first return to Anfield since 2013.

As he walked out of the tunnel he couldn't have failed to notice a new banner high in the Sir Kenny Dalglish Stand. 'LIVERPOOL FC – CHAMPIONS AGAIN,' it read, with a similar one placed on the Kop.

Amazingly, since it was announced in May 2017 that the Centenary Stand would be renamed after King Kenny, the Reds hadn't lost a single Premier League game at Anfield. That wasn't about to change against Villa.

Divock Origi's new bleach-blond haircut was the only highlight of a forgettable first-half before Naby Keita finally unlocked the visitors' defence, teeing up Sadio Mane to slam his 50th goal for Liverpool at Anfield in off the underside of the crossbar.

Curtis Jones, on as a substitute, had signed a new long-term contract 24 hours earlier, calling it "massive," and the 19-year-old made it a weekend to remember when he scored Liverpool's second and his own first Premier League goal.

Curtis was two-and-a-half months old when Reina made his Anfield debut (with Barcelona) in 2001.

Jones also became the 17th different Red to net a league goal in 2019/20, equalling the club record set in 1911/12 and 2015/16, while the last teenager to score a Premier League goal for Liverpool at Anfield was the other 'Scouser in our team', Trent Alexander-Arnold, back in December 2017.

A day later another teenager, Harvey Elliott, put pen to paper on his first professional contract. "Since the day I walked in, it's been an indescribable journey," he said. "I'm just excited to give everything for the club and the fans."

Two new contracts in three days and now a third match in six with a trip to Brighton & Hove Albion, and against the Seagulls it was Liverpool doing the swooping.

Six minutes had gone when Brighton tried to play out from the back only for Keita to nick the ball and slip it to Salah, who found the net.

Just 127 seconds later Jordan Henderson pressed his opponent into an error, received the ball via Keita, Firmino and Salah, and clipped home from 25 yards.

Leandro Trossard got a goal back for the hosts, after earlier being denied by a fine block from Neco Williams who started his first Premier League game at left-back, but Salah made the game safe when he headed home Andy Robertson's corner at the near-post to register his 19th league goal of the campaign.

"We trained [that move] yesterday – and finally Robbo gave me an assist so I'm happy for that!" laughed Mo afterwards, although he should really have left the AMEX with the match-ball after missing a couple of late hat-trick-clinching chances.

The 3-1 victory took the Reds past the 90-points barrier for the second successive season, but it was the end of Henderson's campaign. Forced off with a knee injury, it was initially feared he wouldn't be able to do the famous 'Hendo shuffle' or lift the Premier League trophy. But a scan showed he'd only be out for around six weeks.

Not since 1891/92, the season before Liverpool FC was formed, had a club won every home game in a top-flight season. That was Sunderland, managed by Tom Watson, who would later lead the Reds to their first two First Division titles in 1901 and 1906.

Ahead of welcoming Burnley, the Reds had won 17 out of 17 at Anfield, two of those behind-closed-doors. The clean-sweep was on, but Clarets keeper Nick Pope had other ideas.

Pope made eight saves, two of them world-class from Salah and Mane, to keep Liverpool down to just the one goal, a brilliant first-half header by Andy Robertson from Fabinho's cross. Robbo was denied what looked a stonewall penalty late on when fouled by Johann Gudmundsson, but by then Jay Rodriguez had equalised.

Gudmundsson almost grabbed a shock late winner, crashing a shot against the bar, but the point ended Liverpool's English record of 24 consecutive top-flight home league victories. It was also the first time the Reds had failed to win after scoring first in the Premier League all season.

"For moments it was Liverpool against Pope – he did really well – but we should have scored," said Klopp. "We didn't close the game and they took their moment. It feels like we lost."

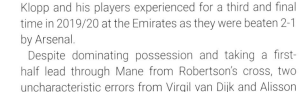

That feeling had been a rarity, but it was something Klopp and his players experienced for a third and final time in 2019/20 at the Emirates as they were beaten 2-1 by Arsenal.

Despite dominating possession and taking a first-half lead through Mane from Robertson's cross, two uncharacteristic errors from Virgil van Dijk and Alisson saw the Gunners lead 2-1 at half-time.

The Reds produced 24 shots to Arsenal's three but could not find a second goal. The defeat meant they could no longer match or overtake Manchester City's record Premier League points tally of 100 points.

There had been much talk of beating that record, yet it was never a target for Klopp and his players. Their aim was simple: win the Premier League. And finally, after 30 years, the moment when Liverpool FC would receive the trophy was here, albeit in circumstances than no one could have envisaged.

"As much as the 90 minutes is the main focus, I

cannot ignore the hugely significant night we are about to experience as a team and a club," wrote Klopp in his Liverpool versus Chelsea matchday programme notes.

"We have enjoyed a wonderful season and it is important we finish it in a manner fitting of the achievement.

"When the game is done, we will be recognised as the Champions of England. The first time since 1990 for this incredible football club. It is so important to enjoy the wonderful moments when they come. And this is one of those."

Had the coronavirus pandemic never happened, the Reds would have received the trophy inside a packed Anfield with a podium constructed on the pitch. But with the title wrapped up with seven games to play, and supporters not permitted inside, Liverpool took the podium to the Kop.

Purple in colour and complete with hand-sanitiser station and social-distancing markers, it was constructed on the most famous stand in football.

The Kop is the heartbeat of Liverpool Football Club. All the great Anfield nights have been played to its cacophony of noise and kaleidoscope of colour.

It has also hosted many hugely emotional Hillsborough

Memorial Services, so it felt right for Sir Kenny Dalglish, the club's last title-winning manager, who was there on that awful day in April 1989, to hand the Premier League trophy over to Henderson.

First, though, there was a game of football to win. With Frank Lampard's Chelsea chasing Champions League qualification, a competitive contest was anticipated. It turned out to be the most intense, exciting, goal-filled game that the Redmen played behind-closed-doors.

Before kick-off, as Sky Sports pundits Graeme Souness and John Barnes narrowly missed a soaking by an Anfield sprinkler, Alex Oxlade-Chamberlain was nutmegged by Xherdan Shaqiri as the Liverpool substitutes warmed up with a 'rondo'. The sound of the subs' laughter echoed around the Main Stand, but it would be the Ox who had the last laugh.

Following another guard-of-honour for the champions – something Chelsea first gave to Bill Shankly's Liverpool at Anfield in 1966 – it was Keita who got the party started.

The opening 20 minutes were cagey as both sides sized each other up, but Naby landed the first punch with a howitzer of a strike from outside the area that clattered into the net via the underside of the bar.

Kepa Arrizabalaga didn't lay a glove on it and the Chelsea keeper didn't even dive for Liverpool's second.

A disputed foul by Mateo Kovacic on Mane sparked some debate between the two benches, but there was no disputing who would take the set-piece. Back in September, during Liverpool's 2-1 win at Stamford Bridge, full-back Trent Alexander-Arnold had scored spectacularly from a free-kick.

This one happened to be about five yards further out, in a similar spot from where Trent had netted against Crystal Palace at Anfield more recently, and the outcome was exactly the same. Right-foot. Top bin. Goal.

It was three a couple of minutes before half-time. Jorginho appeared to handle Robertson's corner, but as Salah appealed for a penalty he also had the presence of mind to flick the ball to Gini Wijnaldum, who volleyed into the roof of the net for Liverpool's 50th Premier League goal of the season at Anfield.

The Reds were cruising, but a reminder of Chelsea's attacking prowess came on the stroke of half-time when Alisson made a stunning one-handed save from Willian only for Olivier Giroud to react first to slide the ball in.

Salah, who needed a goal to become the first Liverpool

player since Roger Hunt to net 20 in the league for three consecutive seasons, had two golden opportunities early in the second half but uncharacteristically miscued both shots.

If it wasn't quite his night, the same couldn't be said about Roberto Firmino.

While not a single Red doubts Bobby's importance to the team, a statistic of failing to score in all 19 of Liverpool's home games is one he'd wanted to avoid.

Had VAR not harshly disallowed his goal against Manchester United in January it would never have been a talking-point. The video assistant referee wasn't about to steal his thunder against Chelsea.

Trent's cross from the right was so precise that you'd swear his right boot comes with laser-guided technology. The ball was inviting Firmino to head it and his RSVP was a firm header into the Kop net, right in front of the podium.

The cheers from the Liverpool bench and even members of the press were so loud you could hear them above the fireworks booming outside. Bobby celebrated with his trademark mid-air kung-fu kick before his team-mates engulfed him. It was also Alexander-Arnold's 13th assist of the season, breaking his own Premier League record for the most goals created by a defender.

Chelsea could have capitulated, but the introduction of Christian Pulisic – a player Klopp knows all about having brought him to Borussia Dortmund when he was 16 – livened them up. In the space of 12 minutes the American international set up Tammy Abraham to make it 4-2, missed a clear-cut chance then took advantage of a collision between Van Dijk and Joe Gomez to make it 4-3.

The wry smile that crossed Klopp's face when his former prodigy netted was the look of a man who knew he'd unearthed a talent.

Yet Klopp, with the help of sporting director Michael Edwards plus senior scouts Barry Hunter and Dave Fallows, has also made a succession of good signings as Liverpool boss. Nine of them – Alisson, Robertson, van Dijk, Fabinho, Wijnaldum, Keita, Firmino, Mane and Salah – started against Chelsea while a tenth came on to seal a 5-3 win with a classic goal on the counter-attack.

Robertson cleared a corner at the near-post with his head, Alexander-Arnold nodded it to Curtis Jones, who gave it to Mane in space on the left.

Sadio looked up and saw Robbo's lung-busting diagonal run from right-back to left-winger.

Mane played the ball down the left. Robertson flew past Jorginho and curled a low cross into the box that Jones let run behind him for Oxlade-Chamberlain to guide a first-time shot with his instep into the net. Poetry. In. Motion.

The full-time whistle signalled the end of a remarkable, unique, home campaign in which the Reds equalled the Premier League record for most points (55) taken on their own turf in a single season.

Liverpool had also gone a club-record third full league season without losing a game at Anfield. Most poignantly of all, the 5-3 victory meant the Reds would receive the Premier League trophy while on 96 points.

"I don't believe too much in coincidences in life, to be honest," admitted Klopp the following day. "I didn't realise directly after the game. I think it was Trent, if I'm right, who saw the 96 points.

"In that moment I really felt it so massively, that things came together in this moment. And I said it after the game that we did it for our supporters, but it cannot be a coincidence that we had 96 points on the night that we got the trophy.

"I hope all the families felt it exactly the same way. It made it really special one more time in that moment."

Liverpool's players momentarily returned to the dressing-room to get changed into special replica shirts with the FIFA Club World Champions badge on the front and 'CHAMPIONS 2019/20' on the back above an image of the Premier League trophy.

Henderson blasted out the players' unofficial title-winning anthem *Show Me Love* as champagne was sprayed amid much bouncing and hugging. Klopp then went round the dressing-room one-by-one.

"What you have done is absolutely outstanding," he

bellowed. "Each of you has made history. Champions of Europe. Champions of the world. Champions of England."

His players responded by dancing around the dressing-room singing 'Campeones, Campeones, Olé, Olé, Olé! – a scene no doubt reflected in many a living-room, garden, street and pub all over the world as Reds supporters celebrated.

Salah, Firmino and Dejan Lovren sprayed their hair red. Wijnaldum and Firmino got out their shades. Most of the players grabbed their phones. Trophy-lifts are on Instagram live these days.

Back outside, the voice of Anfield – stadium announcer George Sephton, who took the job in August 1971 when Liverpool had 'only' won seven league titles – had a classic playlist lined up. *Imagine* by John Lennon, was followed by Queen's *We Are The Champions* which had been regularly played back in the stellar 1970s and 80s.

Other tunes followed as 200 members of the players'

and coaches' families, plus some Melwood staff, were granted special dispensation to watch the trophy-lift from the Main Stand middle tier, provided they adhered to strict COVID-19 protocol.

"That made it really, really special," said the Liverpool manager. "They couldn't watch the game [from the seats] in the stadium, but they were all waiting in different places, waiting for the moment they could come out.

"Then sitting there, seeing their loved ones down there in a very special moment for all of us, that made it absolutely extraordinary. Everybody who was involved in that, who made it happen and organised all the things around, I couldn't thank more."

In April 2017, for a midweek Premier League game against Bournemouth, Sir Kenny Dalglish had sat on the Kop, later revealing "It was just something I wanted to do – it was the first time I've watched a game from there."

Liverpool drew that game 2-2, dropping points as they battled to finish in the top four. Three years and three months later, with Liverpool 18 points clear at the top and champions for 27 days, Kenny was back on the Kop.

This time he was wearing a red face-mask and carrying a large silver trophy alongside Premier League chief executive Richard Masters. The trophy weighs 25.4kg, around four stone. The base, made of the semi-precious stone malachite whose green colour represents the field of play, accounts for 15.9kg.

The weight of expectation when you play for Liverpool and the club hasn't won the title for 30 years is much heavier. But when Dalglish placed the red-ribboned trophy – freshly engraved with '2019-20 LIVERPOOL' – onto a pedestal in the corner of the podium, that weight lifted. Tonight was the night.

With Kanye West's *All of the Lights* playing in the background and LFC TV's Peter McDowall doing the introductions, it was Klopp – wearing a baseball cap and with a red scarf tied around his right arm – who walked up the steps first to receive his golden winners' medal and have a little hug with Dalglish.

Not all of his backroom staff could go on the podium, the majority congregating on the pitch. But joining Klopp were assistant-managers Peter Krawietz and Pep Lijnders, goalkeeping coach John Achterberg and his assistant Jack Robinson, plus elite development coach Vitor Matos, who only joined the club in October.

Andy Lonergan, Caoimhin Kelleher and Harvey Elliott, who hadn't played enough games to qualify for guaranteed medals, followed them.

As dry-ice was pumped into the Kop, with the floodlights switched off and giant spotlights switched on to make Anfield glow red, the 2019/20 Premier

League champions emerged from the Kop concourse one-by-one.

Alisson. Adrian. Virgil van Dijk. Roberto Firmino. Fabinho. Gini Wijnaldum. Sadio Mane. Naby Keita. Joe Gomez. Divock Origi. Alex Oxlade-Chamberlain. Trent Alexander-Arnold. Andy Robertson. James Milner. Adam Lallana. Dejan Lovren. Mo Salah. Joel Matip. Takumi Minamino. Xherdan Shaqiri. Neco Williams. Curtis Jones. Jordan Henderson. In that exact order.

Each took a medal, and as Henderson edged his way towards the trophy, Dalglish – who'd signed the midfield dynamo nine years earlier – gave him a wink.

Jordan collected his medal, placed his hands and lips on the trophy – one kiss is all it takes – and carried it towards his team-mates, who waved their arms and let out a big 'Ooooooh' in anticipation.

The knee-ligament damage suffered at Brighton wasn't about to stop the famous 'Hendo Shuffle' and after quickening the speed of his feet while facing his team-mates, he turned on a sixpence and lifted the trophy high.

It was a moment every Red will re-play over and over again in their minds, never mind on TV or YouTube.

CHAMPIONS!

As the players bounced on the podium, Coldplay's *A Sky Full of Stars* rang out amid a monsoon of red-and-silver ticker-tape and spectacular display of fireworks.

Boom! As somebody once said.

Images representing the Owen McVeigh Foundation and Fans Supporting Foodbanks were beamed onto the pitch as each player and coaching-team member took their turn to lift the trophy before it was brought down to the pitch where they stood together, arm in arm, singing *You'll Never Walk Alone.*

It was Klopp who proudly carried the trophy down the tunnel. "It was absolutely great," he said. "I have to say, the people who organised it made the best of it.

"If it would have been the last game – win today and we are champions – then we wouldn't have had the opportunity to go on the Kop.

"I was never on the Kop before, it was pretty special and I think it makes sense in the moment when the people are not there that we use the Kop to celebrate with them in our hearts."

A couple of days later, Liverpool's first title-winning skipper since Alan Hansen in 1990 was named as the Football Writers' Association Footballer of the Year.

It was the 14th time a Reds player had won the prestigious prize but Jordan Henderson wanted to share it with his team-mates.

"As grateful as I am, I don't feel like I can accept this on my own," he said. "I don't feel like anything I've achieved this season or in fact during my whole career has been done on my own.

"I owe a lot to so many different people but none more so than my current team-mates who have just been incredible and deserve this every bit as much as I do."

Jordan, whose image also appeared in a stunning new piece of street-art opposite Trent's mural off Anfield Road, continued: "We've only achieved what we've achieved because every single member of our squad has been brilliant – and not just in matches, not just in producing the moments that make the headlines but every day in training.

"These lads have made me a better player, a better leader and a better person."

The Reds still had one final game to play, up at Newcastle United, but it wouldn't involve Adam Lallana or Dejan Lovren. Unused substitutes against Chelsea, both gave emotional farewell interviews ahead of moves to Brighton and Zenit St Petersburg respectively.

"My six years have gone in a flash," a tearful Lallana told LFC TV. "My two kids have grown up in Liverpool, it's all they know. I've not just built friends and team-mates here, I've built friends that I see as family forever and that's where the sadness comes from."

Lovren, the first Croatian to win the Premier League, also departed after six years at Anfield. "It was always a dream to come here and leave some footsteps," he said. "It's fantastic to be just a part of this club and I will carry all these moments forever.

"To give everything, and that supporters can say I gave 100 per cent for this club, this means more than anything to me."

A 3-1 win at St James' Park would add a few more records to Liverpool's collection. But after 26 seconds an old adversary, Dwight Gayle, put the Magpies ahead. It was the quickest goal Liverpool had ever conceded in a Premier League game, but this time former Crystal Palace attacker Gayle was on the receiving end of a comeback.

Newcastle didn't touch the ball again in Alisson's penalty area for the rest of the half, which finished 1-1 after Van Dijk headed in Oxlade-Chamberlain's cross. It was the fifth goal of the season for the big Dutchman.

Robertson created Liverpool's second with a new personal-best 12th league assist of the season. The Scotland captain knocked Van Dijk's cross-field pass into the direction of Origi, who cut inside and fired a powerful shot into the bottom corner. Would another season end with Origi having the final say? Not quite.

Klopp made possibly the most frightening substitutions in Premier League history when he brought Firmino, Mane and Salah on at the same time. Magpies boss Steve Bruce didn't know whether to laugh or cry.

Salah struck the post, from Firmino's pass, with his second touch and it was Bobby who created the Reds' 85th and final Premier League goal of the season when he slipped a pass to Mane, who cut inside the area and found the net. It took Liverpool onto a new record points tally of 99, the second-highest ever achieved by any club in the history of top-flight English football. And there was still another piece of silverware to come.

League Titles
19
European Cu
UEFA Champio
League
UEFA Cups
3
L.F.C.

Cups

UEFA
Super Cups

FIFA Club
World Cup

4   1

The following day Klopp was officially named as the 2019/20 League Manager's Association Manager of the Year.

"I am absolutely delighted to get this wonderful trophy," he said. "I have to say thank-you to a lot of people. Sometimes I think it sounds like we have to say it, but it's easy in my case: I am here on behalf of my coaches.

"I said it a lot of times, that I'm okay as a manager but they make me, they make us, a really special bunch of football brains. To work together with Pep Lijnders, Peter Krawietz, John Achterberg, Vitor Matos and Jack Robinson, it's a pleasure.

"I could carry on with the list forever because we have so many great people here who made it happen that this year we won the title, and I only got this trophy because of that, I know. My players, all the people that I work with, I take this and love it for all of us together.

"A very special season with a very special award in the end. Thank you."

Klopp posed for photos with the award and his coaching staff, at Melwood. Behind him, the 'Champions Wall' had been updated for the third time this season.

The Football League trophy silhouette now had the Premier League trophy alongside it. Underneath the words 'League Titles' the number had – finally – changed from 18 to 19.

Job done. Title won. But far from the end of this brilliant Liverpool team's journey.

JULY AWARDS

FWA footballer of the year: **Jordan Henderson**
LMA manager of the year: **Jürgen Klopp**

PREMIER LEAGUE TABLE 26/07/2020

	P	W	D	L	F	A	GD	Pts
Liverpool	38	32	3	3	85	33	52	99
Manchester City	38	26	3	9	102	35	67	81
Manchester United	38	18	12	8	66	36	30	66
Chelsea	38	20	6	12	69	54	15	66
Leicester City	38	18	8	12	67	41	26	62
Tottenham Hotspur	38	16	11	11	61	47	14	59
Wolves	38	15	14	9	51	40	11	59
Arsenal	38	14	14	10	56	48	8	56
Sheffield United	38	14	12	12	39	39	0	54
Burnley	38	15	9	14	43	50	-7	54
Southampton	38	15	7	16	51	60	-9	52
Everton	38	13	10	15	44	56	-12	49
Newcastle United	38	11	11	16	38	58	-20	44
Crystal Palace	38	11	10	17	31	50	-19	43
Brighton	38	9	14	15	39	54	-15	41
West Ham United	38	10	9	19	49	62	-13	39
Aston Villa	38	9	8	21	41	67	-26	35
Bournemouth	38	9	7	22	40	65	-25	34
Watford	38	8	10	20	36	64	-28	34
Norwich City	38	5	6	27	26	75	-49	21

WE BELIEVED

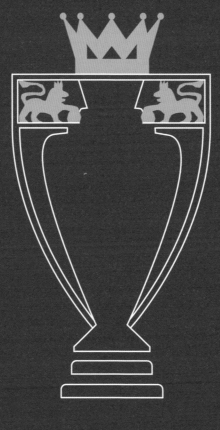

EPILOGUE

THE NORMAL ONE TO CHAMPIONS OF EVERYTHING IN FIVE YEARS

Peter Moore, who stepped down as the club's chief executive officer at the end of August 2020, once described Jürgen Klopp as "one of the more holistic human beings you will ever meet...even when you have lost he makes you think there is brighter sunshine ahead."

Days after the title triumph the manager was the subject of a Channel 4 documentary entitled *Germany's Greatest Export* which chronicled his early career through to his effortlessly charming, utterly disarming entrance at Anfield in October 2015 when he described the club's history as legendary but also as a "twenty-kilo backpack", promised to bring "emotional football" to LFC and predicted: "If we sit here in four years, I think we win one title."

Towards the end of the 2019/20 season, matchday programme columnist and former Reds title-winner Gary Gillespie paid his own tribute: "You have to have a fit with a football club and the affinity between him and Liverpool is perfect. It was the same when he was with Mainz and then with Borussia Dortmund.

"Klopp's style of play suits the Liverpool philosophy. He's galvanised the players and the whole club. He gets the best out of everyone and has them pulling in the right direction."

Gillespie added that "a lot of credit goes to the owners too. It's all in place behind the scenes. The stadium is magnificent, there's a brand new training ground on the way, the backroom staff are world-class, but first and foremost you have to do it on the pitch – and the players have done just that.

"It's never easy to defend a title and there is a big task ahead next season. But this club is in a really good place."

Four major – major – trophies won in just over 12 months. Premier League champions in the most extraordinary season ever. A team packed full of modern LFC legends, fearless and flamboyant, smashing records and setting the bar ever higher.

Ninety-nine points, a new club record along with most wins (32), most away victories (14) and most league 'doubles' (13). Eighteen points clear of the field, a staggering 33 ahead of the team in third-place.

Klopp again: "It started on 1 June 2019 [after the Champions League final] because yes, that was the last game of the last season, but for us, it was pretty much the first game of a pretty special time.

"So after that the Super Cup, the Club World Cup and now the Premier League is absolutely exceptional. The football part of the year was exceptional, absolutely exceptional.

"Ninety-nine points after having 97 last year. The boys have shown a consistency which is really second-to-none, and that's what we had to do – we knew that."

Right-back Trent Alexander-Arnold, a multiple trophy-winner and still only 21, told LFC TV that it was down to "the whole club, the way it's run and our beliefs.

"It's the players, the manager, the coaches, the staff, pulling together to be able to achieve these things with the fans. We've waited so long and we've been able to do it.

"We're really proud as a team and I'm proud to be able to see everyone in the city so happy – well, all the

Liverpool fans obviously! It's a proud moment for the club."

This was also a win for those who'd come close over previous seasons. Liverpool had also been runners-up under Gerard Houllier in 2001/02, with Rafael Benitez in 2008/09, Brendan Rodgers in 2013/14, Klopp himself in 2018/19.

Three of those near-misses featured Steven Gerrard, arguably the greatest midfielder of his generation. Right player, right club, not quite – agonisingly – the right time.

The last word goes to the main man, writing in his manager's programme notes for the final home fixture of 2019/20 against Chelsea, with the red-ribboned trophy ready to be presented.

"This is our moment – we have all earned it. So embrace it and cherish it."

SCROLL OF HONOUR

THE MANAGER, STAFF & PLAYERS

JÜRGEN **KLOPP**
PETER **KRAWIETZ**
PEPIJN **LIJNDERS**
JOHN **ACHTERBERG**
JACK **ROBINSON**
VITOR **MATOS**
NEIL **CRITCHLEY**
ANDREAS **KORNMAYER**
ANDREW **MASSEY**
PHILIPP **JACOBSEN**
CONALL **MURTAGH**
TOM **KING**

JORDAN **FAIRCLOUGH**
PAUL **SMALL**
LEE **RADCLIFFE**
GRAHAM **CARTER**
DAVID **RYDINGS**
MONA **NEMMER**
MARK **LEYLAND**
GREG **MATHIESON**
JAMES **FRENCH**
JOSE LUIS **RODRIGUEZ**
RICHIE **PARTRIDGE**
JOE **LEWIS**

ALISSON **BECKER**
FABINHO
VIRGIL **VAN DIJK**
GEORGINIO **WIJNALDUM**
DEJAN **LOVREN**
JAMES **MILNER**
NABY **KEITA**
ROBERTO **FIRMINO**
SADIO **MANE**
MOHAMED **SALAH**
JOE **GOMEZ**
ADRIAN
JORDAN **HENDERSON**

ALEX **OXLADE-CHAMBERLAIN**
TAKUMI **MINAMINO**
ADAM **LALLANA**
ANDY **LONERGAN**
XHERDAN **SHAQIRI**
ANDY **ROBERTSON**
DIVOCK **ORIGI**
JOEL **MATIP**
CURTIS **JONES**
CAOIMHIN **KELLEHER**
TRENT **ALEXANDER-ARNOLD**
HARVEY **ELLIOTT**
NECO **WILLIAMS**

Fahmi Abas
Gary Abbott
Michael Abboud
Fakhzan Syah Abdul Rahim
John Paul Abrahams
Brian Adelgaard
Claudia Bram Alfie Erin
Calvin Alimo
Andrew Allen
Kirsty, David & Joshua Allman
Craig Allred
Arjun Amin
Kanorkorn Ananchotikul
Osten Andersson
Lengderson Ang LH
Ken Ankers
Martin Ankers
Ray Annal
Dave Aplin
Wayne Appleton
Khanit Aramkitpota
Raymond Arthur
Eden Asfaw
Greg Ashcroft
Macaulay Ashton
Ken Ashun
Lauren Ashun
Lee Ashun
Harri Aston
Mark Aulton
Gareth Aylott
James Ayres
Mark Baker
Andrew Thomas Banks
Simon Banstead
Simon Baptist
Farooq Bapu
Ryan Barker
Alison Barkley
Anthony Barkley
Elliot James Barkley
Sophia Autumn Barkley
Mark Barnard
John Paul Barrett
Jason Bartlett
Samuel Bartlett
Okcan Basat
Steven Bates
James Beaney
Maik Bedziecha
Kim Beer
Bernadette Bennett

Harrison Bennett
John Bennett
Stephen Benns
Frank Bernardino
Robbie Besana
Susan Biedla
Andrew Birchall
Andy Birchall
Bob Birchall
Tim Bird
Kevin Blackwell
Matt Bloor
Aimelie Bluck
Peter Bluck
Shevrik Bluck
Manjeet Boall
Zachary Boardman
Sean Bocking
Suthikiat Boonpensilp
Pornthep Boonyaman
Jan Borkowski
Jonathan Borland
Sittichai Borrisuttanakul
Tim Bouquet
Damien Boyle
Steven Braden
Brandon-Paul Bradley
Brody-Francis Bradley
David Bradley
John Bradley
Johannes Bragi Gislason
Danny Brennan
Jeanette Brennan
Jonathon Brennan
Patrick Brickley
Adrian Broadbent
Tom Broadfoot
Max & Beau Brodrick
Paul Brooks
Isaac Broome
Christine Brown
Claire Brown
Graham Brown
James John Brown
Jenny Brown
Michael Brown
Ben Browning
Antonia Bruna Justo
Geraint Bryant
Rebecca Buchanan
Mark Buckley
Freddie Burnie

Anne Burns	Gwenyth Chia SG	Tony Crowley	Alun (Twins) a Rich Efans	Haslan Farouk Fuad
Chad Burns	Henry Chin	John Culshaw	Stephen Egan	Faith Fulcher
Evie Burns	Pichate (Joe) Chinaramrungruang	Eugene Cunningham	Sigurdur Einar Einarsson	Nane Gällros
Iola Burns	Kuda Chirewa	William Cunningham	Peter Eldred	Judith and Pamela Gardiner
Ivy Burns	Sumphan Chitwilai	Triffin Dalikouras	Matt Ellery	Michael Gardiner
Joanne Burns	Charnchai Chokchaipitak	Brian Dangerfield	Riley Ellery	Francis Gardler
Lacey Burns	Oliver Chow	Mark Daniels	Andrew Hartley Elliott	Terence Garland
Lewis Burns	Samuel Chow	Terry Danks	Richard Ellis	Jasper Gartrell-David
Luke Burns	Lars Christensen	Ryan Darbyshire	Steve Ellis	Liam Garvey
Lydia Burns	Hubert Cini	Adam Daulby	Steve Ellis	Sean Garvey
Lynne Burns	Michael Christopher Clark	Jackie Daulby	Tito Elstinovic	Tim Gately
Maisie Burns	Tyler Clark	Bernard Davies	Jose Fernando Estrada Gallo	Jason Gates
Michael Burns	Aria Rae Clarke	Chris Davies	Sam Etheridge	Roy Gates
Brian Burrows	Elliott-James Clarke	Frank Davies	Bronwen Margaret Evans	Reto Genini
Estelle Buscombe	Sam David George Clynch	Huw Davies	Katie Evans	Steven Gerrard
Bernie Butchard	Jimmy Coffey	Joe Davies	Luke Daniel Evans	Manjinder Ghuman
Lloyd Butler	Keith Coker	Kyle Davies	Manon Evans	Kenny Giles
Pete Butler	Steven Coldbeck	Martin Davies	Ellis Evison	Aaron Gilfoyle
Thomas Butlin	James Coleiro	Ricki Davies	Craig Faill	Alison Gilfoyle
Eden Butterworth	Jack Coleman	Rob Davies	David Fairhurst	Bethany Gilfoyle
Terry Byrne	Brian Gerald & Matthew Collins	Tom Davies	Kusabs Family	Carmen Gilfoyle
Ariel Manuel D. Cabatbat	Kian Collins	Adrian Davis	Martyn Farrell	Carol Gilfoyle
Bob Caddick	Sheldon Helen Harry Deanna	Tony Davis	Alex, Liam & Jacob Fasting	Connor Gilfoyle
Paul Cadman	Collins YNWA	Graham Daws	Bernie Feeney	Holly Gilfoyle
Daniel Callon	Graham Colvin	Chris De Silva	Nick Fellows	Kevin Gilfoyle
Matthew Callon	Gavin Conlan	Raphael Defreitas	Will Fenton	Roy Gilfoyle
Elaine Calpin	Joe Connolly	Rick Del Rio	Robert Ferris	Sam Gilfoyle
Elias Oscar Camenzind	Colin Connor	Erick Dela Rosa	Ian Fidler	William Gilfoyle
Michael Cameron	Ronnie Cooke	Shane Delaney	Angela Finch	Brandy Gilleece
Scott Campbell	John Coombs	Jake Demasi	George Eric Findlay	Alan James Gilliland
Jason Carew	Paul Cooper	Ernie Dempster	Eugene Finn	Valerie Gilliland
Paul Jack Carine	Paul Corbyn	Adam Devet	Matthew Finney	Josiah Goh
Matthew Carn	Padraig Corduff	Tim Dible	Carl Fisher	Mark Goodwin
Michael Carr	Mick Corns	Peter Dojcsan	Mark Fisher	David Gordon
Terry Carter	Geoffrey Costo	Billy Dolan	Paul Fisher	Dave Gould
Tony Carter	Henry Costo	Louie Dolan	Paul Fisher	Aaron Gouthwaite
Chris Carver	Stan Cottrell	Marc Douwen	Charles Fitzell	Alessandra Lucia Gouthwaite
Roberto Casado	Sophia Coughlan	Tony Downes	John Fitzpatrick	Cayden-Paul Gouthwaite
Jamie Castley	Kevin Cowley	Stuart Drewery	Molly Flanagan	Geoff Gouthwaite
Shea Castley	Liam Cox	Iain Duffy	Andy Flint	Les Gouthwaite
Steve Catley	Paul Cox	Rob Duffy	BJ Augustine Fong	Paul Gouthwaite
Joshua Catten	Albert Stanley Cragg	James Duke	Kim Fong	Stacey Gouthwaite
Dave Cattermole	Arron Craw	Marcus Dunne	Joseph Formosa (Il-Forie)	Harold Gouthwaite Jnr
Keylie Cavanagh	Karen Crawley	Lewis Dye	Eric Forsyth	Harold Gouthwaite Snr
Lim Chai Teck	Kevin Crewe Snr	Mark Dymond	Jonathan Fowler	Alun Grace
Angus Chan	John Critchley	Kevin Eccles	Ollie Fowler	Connagh Grace
CY Chan	Lisa Critchley	Fred Eccleston	Tom Fowler	Gary Grace
Aylwin Chee	Lynda Critchley	Paul Eccleston	Barrie Fowles	Dennis Graham
Shelley Cheeseman	Kenneth Crompton	Lin Junxiang: Eddy	Gordon France	Harry Graham
Leroy Chen	Matthew Cronin	Jonathan Edge	OLSC France	Jay Graham
Ryk Chew	Luke Croucher	Nick, Mandy, Rhys, Megan Edwards	Katie Francis	Jennifer Graham
Han Keong Chia	Tafara Crowder		Angus Freeman	Mary Grealey

THE FANS

Ady Green
Roger Greenberg
Jamie Greenwood
Corey Gregson
Robert Grenda
Amandeep Grewal
Brian, Chloe & Grace Griffiths
Richard Griffiths
Pamela Grys
Brian Gunning
Brian Thomas Gunning
Derek Haines
Harvey Haines
Jean Haines
Neil Haines
Lucas Hale
Colin James Hall
Elliot Halligan
Lucas Halligan
Gillian Hallowell
Inkatuuli Haltsonen
Henry Eileen Han
Paul Hanrahan
Sandra Hanrahan
George Hanson
Patrick Haralabidis
Kevin Harker
Nicholette Harper
Derek John Harriott
Carl Harris
Lee Harris
Shaun Harris
Martin Harrison
Martin Harrison
Victoria Hart
Joshua Hartley
Thomas Haslam
Thomas Hatley
Ottar Hauge
Yvonne Hawker
John Haworth
David James Hay
Kevin Hayden
Terry Hayes
Thomas Hayes-Sinclair
Angus Hayward
Charles Hayward
Eleanor Hayward
Georgina Hayward
Richard F Hayward
John Heath
Matt Heath
Sarah Heath
Hollie Hedley
Neil Hedley
Mali Ffion Heighway
Jeroen Heijink

Ola Helgedagsrud
Jeremy Heng
Leo Hentzel
Adam Hewinson
Amy Hill
Darren Hill
Geoff Hill
Jonny Hill
Simon Hill
Torin Hill
Tony Hillman (Kernow Scouser)
Lim Kwan Hin
John Hinchliffe
Harry Hodgkinson
Christopher Hodgson
Lee Hodson
Joseph Holdsworth
Michael Hollan
Shane Holmes
Chuang Hongzhou
Dermot Horan
David Horridge
David Houlgate
Victor JY Huang
Amy Hughes
Caleb Joseph Hughes
Kieran Hughes
Rob Hughes
Tjay Hughes
Gethin Hughes Davies
Joe Hulse
Ian K Humphries
Martin Hunt
Marty Hurl
Stephen Hutchinson
Charlie Hynes
Cormack Hynes
James Hynes
Jimmy Hynes
John Hynes
Molly Hynes
Keita Ishii
Damyan Ivanov
Dylan J
Abe Jacob
Andrew Jeffery
Benny Jensen
Manasa Jerera
Martin Jervis
Aaron "AJ" Johnson
Harry Johnson
Emma Jolliffe
Alexander H Jones
Baby Dean Jones
Bobster Jones
Finley Jones
Heath Jones

Ian (Iant) Wyn Jones
Ian Bones Jones
John Jones
Libby Jones
Maria Ceris Jones
Martin Jones
Megan Jones
Mikey R Jones
Patricia Jones
Peter Jones
Stephanie Jones
Tessa Jones
Yvonne Jones
Will Jones 87
Yannick Jonker
Thea-Maria Sofie Bønsøe
Jørgensen
Anthony Juraga
Ferran Kaharudin
Bardhyl Bob Kallamata
Colin Kangaloo
Bjorn Karlstrom
Harry Kavanagh
Dan Kay
Jonny Kay
Jimmy Keane
Declan Kearns
Curtis Kee
Tony Kehoe
Cameron Keir
Fraser Keir
David Kellner
Thomas Kelly
Michael JF Kemp
Nigel Kemp
Carolyn Kennedy
Peter Austin Kennedy
Robert Kennedy
Ste Kennedy
Ava Kennerley
Harry Kennerley
Paul Kennerley
Sam Kennerley
Jason Kenny
Connor Kenyon
James Kenyon
Carl Keszei
Sandy Singh Khanijou
Mariam Khayrutdinova
Jack Kielty
Tracy Kielty
Gee Syub Kim
Wang Kim Meng
Chris King
Kevin King
Steve King
Bradley Kingham

Ian Kinnear
Sean Lee Kirwan
Jason Kitchen
Chad Klythom
Dave Knox
Tony Knox
Gerard Koh
Aaron Kok
Twist Kongpila
Sara-Ann Krishnamoorthy
Saeed Kronfli
Wieslaw Kula
Sergei Kuznetsov
Aiden Kwan
Jason Kwan
Jayden Kwan
Peksoon Kwan
Andy Lamb
Gary Landry
Fredrik Larsson
Ronald Law
Brion Lawless
Ben Lawrence
Chris Lawrence
Dan Lawrence
Alistair Lee
Gary Lee
Anthony Lee Chee Choong
Rhianna Ami-Jade Lees
Simon Lees
Vichyathon Lertwongweerachai
Waratorn Lertwongweerachai
Paul Leunissen
Max and Amélie Lewens
Dwight Lewis
Paul Jacob Luke Lewis
Jenny Lewton
Boon Keat Lian
Kahchi Liew
John Lightfoot
Euan & Min Yu Lim
Nivel Lim
Su Chwee Lim
Kelvin Heike Lim Yyan Xi
Dag Lindholm
Beth Lindop
Louise Lloyd
Kay Lindsay
Mikkel Linneberg
Ian Littlewood
Wayne Littlewood
Noah Calvin Trent Liu Man Hin
Louise Lloyd
Simon K Lloyd
Moi Jon Lloyd-Davies
Eleanor Yuen Sum Lo
Peter Locke
Esther Lois

Suvipavee Loke-witaya
Peter Lomas
Michael Longauer
Nick Longauer
Keith Longworth
Chun Fai Loo
Alistair Lord
Håkan Lövström
Kelvin Low
Patrick Lucas
Bob Lund
Jonny Lund
Ben Lynch
Matthew MacKenna
Seamus MacKenna
Justin Maclean
Scott Maclean
Lola Macmichael
Joe Magee
Keith Magill
Dan Main
Andrew Major
Jonevir Malabuyoc
Ioan Ray Mali-mae
Yoav Malka
Shaun Anthony Maloney
Matt Mangan
Alan Robert Joel Lucy Mannering
Damien Mannion
Emma Mansfield
Gauti Arnar Marinósson
Andy Marsden
Ben Marsden
Rebecca Marsh
Frank Martin
Phil Martin
Joe Martinex
Adam Mason
Alby Mason
Alwyn Mason
Arlo Mason
James Mason
James Mason
Oscar Masters
Palle Matthiasen
Gerry May
Tom McAuliffe
Alfie Mcavoy
Eamonn McBride
Linda McCann
Rachel McCann
Daniel McChrystal Plimmer
Harry McConnachie
Matthew McConville
Stephen McCreery
Elizabeth McCulloch
Joe McCulloch

Joseph McCulloch
Thomas McCulloch
Bobby Mcdonald
David McDowell
John F McDowell
Sandra McGill
John Mcgivern
Martin McGivern
Charlie McGlown
Jack McGowan
Liam McGowan
James McGrath
Gus McGroarty
Wayne McGuigan
Dean McGuinness
Gerry McGuinness
Joyce McGuinness
Samantha McGuinness
Shirley McGuinness
Jamie McKeenan
Cameron McKenzie
Robert McKenzie
Conor McLean
Andy McLoughlin
Christine McLoughlin
Lucy McLoughlin
Prisca McLoughlin
James McMahon
Will McMahon
Andrew McMinn
David McMullan Mak
Ava McNally
Dean McNally
Donna McNally
Harry McNally
Ian McNally
Sean McNally
Soraya Meah
Harry Meijer
Andrew Melia
Reuben Melville
Gopinathan (Pappae) Menon
Nicholas Meredith Davies
Paul Merrifield
Colin Metcalfe
Vanessa Middleton
David Milburn
John Miller
Michael Miller
Scott Mills
Jack Milward
Iain & Louis Minton
Lily Mitchell
Neil and Dan Mobsby
Francis Monaghan
Isaac Monaghan
John Monaghan

Max Monaghan
Ged & Sean Montgomery
Tyrone Montgomery
Jamie Moore
Joe Moore
Rory Moore
Patsy Moran
John Morley
Brin Morris
Bryan Morris
Harry Ioan Morris
Tom Morris YNWA
James Morrison
Jim Morrison
Andrew Morton
Robin Moseley
Robbie Lewis Moslin -Cooke
Barry Moxley
Kayleigh Moylan
Artur Mucha
Danny Mulhearn
Steve Munachen
Nantha Kumar Munisamy
Chetan Murarji
Jasmin Murphy
Laura Murphy
Oscar Murphy
Paul Murphy
Tazio Muschi
Tony Musker
James Muxlow
Maya Myint
Amara Naidoo
Mihir Naidoo
Hema Nair
Yoshitaka Nakamura
Kevin Narramore
Paul Negi
Lesley Nelson
Mike Nelson
Sam Nelson
Nathan Ng
Sam Ng
James Philipp Nicholson
David Nolan
Kenny Nolan
Tom Nunn
Joe Nuttorn
Snorre Andreas Nyeggen
Claudia Oakley
Jacques O'Beirne
Gary O'Connor
Steve O'Donoghue
Barry Darragh Conor O'Keeffe
Arnold Oumo Okiror
Samuel Oumo Okiror
Tayo-Feyin Olatunde

Jack Oliver
Javier Oliver Torrijos
Amari Olok Okiror
Siraj Omar
Paul O'Neill
Shaun O'Neill
Kok Leong Ong
Leonard Ong
Ste O'Reilly
Paul Osborne
Alan O'Toole
Akarach (Chim) Pakarathanitthkul
Steve Pallett
Maya Panasar
Gerald Pang
Bank, Nina, Patrick, Rita
Panyayong
Ben Park
Jesse Parker
Anna Parkinson
Frank Parle
Alexander Parr
Lewis Parr
Sonny Parr
Thomas Parr
Dipesh Patel
Jayesh Patel
Ross Paterson
Maurice Patterson
Susan Pattie
Lynne Paul
Jeff Peace
Matthew Peace
Tilly Peacock
Gregg Pearcey
John Pearcey
Richard Pedder
Charlie Penders
Caius Penfold
Joshua Penfold
Brian Peters
Darren Phillips
Gary Phillips
Michael Phillips
Robert Phinney
Surachest Phornsuwannapha
Apiphop Phungchanchaikul
Andrew Pickett
Rhys Pill
Tony Pinch
Simon Bradley Pinkus
Prasit Pinta
Mark Platt
Blair Pogue
Ethan Pogue
Matthew Pomford
Bertie Poole

Herman Post
Daniel Pound
Andrew Powell
Dave Powell
Eileen Powell
Mark Powell
Sam Powell
Frankie Powell Snr
David Pownall
Chawalit Pradprieo
A. Devin Pranata
Rangga Pratama
Junior Joseph Price
Katie Price
Phil Price
Alan Prideaux
Paul Pritchard
Mark, Caroline, William,
Lydia Prosser
Thomas Wyn Pugh
Petri Puttonen
Osman Qadir
Katja Quaschny
Ralph Quigley
Michael Quinn
Issac Qureshi
Alan Radford
Esme Rae
Thoenix Rafan
Misha Rahman
Tarapong Rakked
Wittaya Raksasat
Ben Ralf
Aditay Raj Rambarran
Robert Ramsey
Chris Randles
Maddie Randles
David Ray
Peter-John Rayfield
MapleLeaf Red
Michelle Redmond
Tracy Rees
Bryony Rees-Winter
Jamie Rees-Winter
Darryl Reeves
Alex Reid
Chris Reid
David Reilly
Keith Rennie
David Neale Reynolds
Dave Ginger Rhyl
William Rice
Joel Richards
Darren Richardson
Carragher Rico
Mark, Jo & Alex Ridout
Piyawat Riendechawetchakul

Patricia Riley
Phil Rimmer
Dillon Ritchie
Joseph Ritchie
Mark Ritchie
Mark Ritchie Jnr
Nick & Chrissie Roberts
Tony Roberts
Ken Robertson
Luke Robertson
Luke Snr Robertson
Louise Robins
Joy Robinson
Robert Rodmell
Rebecca Rodrigues
Oliver Rogers
Andrew Rollins
John Rolo Rollinson
Colin and Jane Rooney
Ben Rorke
Jacob Rorke
Sean Rorke
Mark Roscoe
Ian Ross
Tiziano Rossi
Ellias Round
Joel Round
Peter LFC Tigger Rowan
Mahi Ruhi
Andrea Rule
Waleed Sabawi
John Owen Salkeld
Chafic Salloum
Lim Mook San
Anthony Sanders
Purwinder Sandhu
Rashpal Sandhu
Thirukumaran Sankaran
Pratya Saringkharn (Thai)
David Saunders
Mark Savage
Daniel Noah Schembri
John Scott
Nick Sellars
Zoey Senyszyn
David Sephton
Joshua Sewell
Mark Shale
Jonathan Sharp
Philip Shaw
Elliot Shea
Vikneswaran Sheekar
Daniel Shields
Neil Shillan
Bob Shrubb
Raspal Singh Sidhu
James Siedler

Farel Silalahi
Lorenzo Simm
Alan Simpson
Norman Sin
Nilly Singh
Pinder Singh
Pinna Singh
Richard Singh
Terry Siow
Marut Siriratatsadon
Karol Siskind
Chayanunt Siwarungson
John Kevin Slater
Philippe Sloan
Remi Sloan
HC Sloth
Graeme Small
Sean Smart
Christopher Gareth Smith
Gemma Smith
Jude Smith
Leslie Colin Smith
Madison Smith
Nina Smith
Paul Smith
Tracey Smith
Kieran Smyth
Jarek Sobkowicz
Vijay Solanki
Helge Gunnar Solbakken
Jamal Soliman
Jacky Soo
Jesper Soulbes Hansen
John Sowerby
David John Speed
Harrison Cole Speed
Finlay Spence
Kieran Spillane
Michael Spillane
Peter Spillane
Theo Squires
Claire Standish
Myles Standish
Sadie Standish
Olivia Stanhope
John Martyn Stapley Lopez
The Starmers
Panos Stavrou
Philip Stearn
Arnt Steffensen
Nikos Stefos
Knut Andreas Stenseth
Andy Stephen
Peter Stetefeldt
Ryan Stewart
Douglas Stirling
Euan Stirling

Ivo Stirling
Stuart Stirling
Malcolm Stobbart
Sofia Stobbs
Robert Stocker
Paul Stocks
Don Street
Harry Street
Michael Stuart
Pannathorn-Prapoj Sukmanont
Phil Summerfield
Alana Sumpter
Ben Sumpter
Colin Sumpter
Cerys Sumpter
Debra-Lea Sumpter
Ian Sumpter
Ian George Sumpter
Jake Sumpter
John Sumpter
Katie Sumpter
Kathleen Sumpter
Kevin Sumpter
Nick Sumpter
Paul Sumpter
Natthaphol Suntudkarn
Jason Swinden
Patryk Szmitkowski
David Szpiro
Tom & Victor Szymanski
Daryl Tam
Andrew Tan
Chee Kean Tan
Jack Hann Tan
Stanley Tan YS
James Taylor
Jonathan Taylor

Mark Taylor
Neil Taylor
Roman Taylor-Smith
Ryan Teer
Maverick Teo
Nicholas TGB
Prasart Theerajantranon
Thossapol Themna
Suren Thiru
Andrew Thomas
David Thomas
Victoria Thomas
Helen Thompson
Christopher Thorpe
Timo Tiainen
Christopher Tipping
Kwang Chern Toh
Archie Townley
James Tran
Thanatorn -Lim- Treechanakij
Ashvina Trivedi
King Yiu Tung
Kevin Turner
Brent Twaites
Adam Vailionis
Jos van Beusekom
Leilani van Schouwen
Pat Veach
Scott Veach
Alf Vicary
Tor Henrik Von Der Ohe
Brian Walker
Lewis Walker
Simon Walker
Harry Vera Elaine Gill Wallworth
Bob Walsh
Liam Walsh

Supakij (Kop) Wangdumrongves
Brian Warburton
Craig Warcup
Ewan Ward
Kade Warner
Thomas Waters
Thomas "Tate" Waters
Robert Watkinson
Jacqueline Watson
Emily Watt
Robert Webb
Bradley Welsh
Chris Welsh
Connor Welsh
Gary Welsh
Jamie Welsh
Nick & Shazza Welsh
Rob Welsh
Robyn Welsh
Bradley Welsh Jnr
Marcus Went
Charlie White
Darren White
Leslie White
Steven Whitehead
Adam Whitehouse
Melanie Whitehouse
Clive Whiteside
Peter Whittaker
Samuel James Wignall
Paul Wildridge
Baz Wilkinson
Scott Wilkinson
Cameron Williams
Danny Williams
Daz Williams
Dylan (Wil) Williams

Emma Williams
Ian Williams
Stephen B Williams
Tracy, Neil, Iris Williams
Albie Williamson
Mark Williams-Payne
Matt Wilson
Susan Wilson
Andrew Winder
Michael Winter
Allan Wolff
Doctor Wolfman
The Wols
Steve Wolstenholme
Jaan Mikael Wong
Jonathan Wong
Nelson CC Wong
William Wong
Stephen Woods
Allan Wright
Bradley Wright
Philip Wright
Steven Wright
Megan Wyatt
Tai Tong Xinxian
Patrick Xuereb
Tang Loon Yang
Terence Yap
Cassius Yates
ZM Yeap
Sarah & Jane Yeomans
Jasper Alice Ben Yeung Chi Bun
Edmond Yun
Charles Zahra
Ahmad Zamri
David Zhou
Raina Zhu

The Champions Wall

League Titles	European Cup/ UEFA Champions League	FA Cups	UEFA Cups	League Cups	UEFA Super Cups	FIFA Club World Cup
19	6	7	3	8	4	1